UNIVERSITY OF NORTH CAROLINA
STUDIES IN THE ROMANCE LANGUAGES AND LITERATURES

Number 99

THE REV. JOHN BOWLE
THE GENESIS OF CERVANTEAN CRITICISM

THE REV. JOHN BOWLE
THE GENESIS OF CERVANTEAN CRITICISM

BY

RALPH MERRITT COX

CHAPEL HILL

THE UNIVERSITY OF NORTH CAROLINA PRESS

depósito legal: v. 958 - 1971

artes gráficas soler, s. a. - jávea, 28 - valencia (8) - 1971

CONTENTS

		Pages
	PREFACE	9
I.	Who was John Bowle?	13
II.	"Don Quixote" in the Seventeenth and Eighteenth Centuries	27
III.	The Earliest Manuscript and the Final Form of Bowle's Edition	48
IV.	The Editor's Conception of "Don Quixote"	62
V.	Bowle's General Attitude Toward Cervantes	77
VI.	The Influence of Bowle on Later Cervantean Criticism (1780-1840)	101
	BIBLIOGRAPHY	119

PREFACE

I first became interested in studying literary criticism as it regards Spanish literature a few years ago when, as a beginning graduate student, I made an investigation of the early editions of Garcilaso's poetry. Herrera and El Brocense fascinated me, and the interest they awakened led to more reading and studying of the genre of which their works concerning Garcilaso are supreme examples. It was only natural that I should eventually look into the criticism and editing of *Don Quixote*. When I came upon the name of John Bowle, like most people I had heard nothing about him. As I slowly came to know the Englishman and what he had done, I saw the enormity of the failure to recognize this man who has done so much for Spanish letters. With Bowle we are dealing with one example of a particular genre: commentary. Bowle follows the path set by all those commentators who in the Renaissance and later sought to raise their subjects to heights of renown and authority. Because he is the first to raise Cervantes to eminence, John Bowle is most deserving of study and understanding.

It was disturbing to realize that Bowle, who produced the first truly learned edition of *Don Quixote* and who set up the basis for later editing of the novel, has been relegated to obscurity. Virtually nothing has been written about him, but the few statements that I was able to discover were all in agreement about the intrinsic worth of his edition:

> George Ticknor, *History of Spanish Literature*, III (London, 1849), p. 383: "There are few books of so much real learning, and at the same time of so little pretension, as the third volume of this edition [Bowle's]. It is, in fact,

the true and safe foundation on which has been built much of what has since been done with success for the explanation and illustration of the Don Quixote...."

Leopoldo Rius, *Bibliografía crítica de las obras de Miguel de Cervantes Saavedra*, I (Madrid, 1895), p. 46: "Sus anotaciones son, pues, de gran utilidad en muchos pasajes para declarar la propiedad de las palabras, explicar el verdadero sentido del contexto y averiguar las circunstancias de los dichos y de los hechos; y si bien no se les puede dar nombre de comentario, porque la interpretación se refiere á la letra y no al espíritu ó fondo del *Quijote*, es muy apreciable el minucioso trabajo del doctor Bowle, quien además tiene el mérito de haber sido el primero que llevó á cabo de un modo completo, una empresa tan importante...."

Julio Casares, "Las tres edades del 'Quijote,' " *Boletín de la Real Academia Española, Tomo XXVII* (Madrid, 1948), pp. 43-44: "Como lector ingenuo de Cervantes... me inspiran gratitud aquellos beneméritos varones que pasaron lo mejor de su vida depurando los textos, aclarando pasajes oscuros, ilustrando sucesos olvidados, desentrañando alusiones implícitas, evocando instituciones, costumbres y ambientes desaparecidos y procurándonos, en una palabra, la mejor comprensión de lo que real y verdaderamente escribió el Príncipe de los Ingenios. Me importa esto mucho más que cualquier especulación subjetiva, por aguda e ingeniosa que sea, acerca de lo que no dijo Cervantes.... Doy preferencia, pues, a los 'comentaristas' sobre los 'exegetas,' y creo que es de justicia reservar el primer lugar entre aquéllos al verdadero fundador de la crítica erudita del *Quijote*, al vicario de Idmiston, John Bowle... cuyo nombre, por cierto, no ha merecido en la 'Enciclopedia Británica' el honor de un artículo. Sus famosas 'anotaciones,' discutidas, mejoradas y con harta frecuencia saqueadas por quienes vinieron después, despiertan todavía admiración y pueden estudiarse con fruto."

These statements persuaded me that some kind of general study should be made of Bowle and his work, and a "general study" is precisely what has been attempted in this book. It was thought that since no real work has been done on John Bowle, as comprehensive an investigation as possible should be made of him here. To present this over-all view, I have divided the study into six chapters. The first three give a résumé of Bowle's life, a short history of the criticism of *Don Quixote* before Bowle's edition, and a description of Bowle's work. The next two discuss the editor's attitudes toward *Don Quixote* and Cervantes, and the last is a study of the influence which Bowle's edition had on immediately succeeding commentators of the novel.

I am greatly indebted to several people for their assistance in various ways during the last year and more. To Professors M. J. Benardete, Wallace Fowlie, Mack Singleton, and Bruce Wardropper I would like to express my very deep appreciation.

RALPH MERRITT COX

May, 1969
Durham, North Carolina

I

WHO WAS JOHN BOWLE?

The only source providing any really pertinent data about John Bowle is the *Dictionary of National Biography,* that has a good résumé of his life and gives the principal details of his career fairly concisely. Bowle was born on October 26, 1725, a descendant of Dr. John Bowle, a former Bishop of Rochester during the seventeenth century. He received his degree from Oxford (Oriel College) in 1750, and in 1776 was elected a Fellow of the Society of Antiquaries. Later he received the vicarage of Idmiston (spelled Idemeston in his edition of *Don Quixote*) after having taken orders. He died in Wiltshire on October 26, 1788, his birthday. [1]

In January of 1781, the same year that his edition appeared, Bowle wrote a letter to the *Gentleman's Magazine* concerning Juan Antonio Pellicer's recently published *Noticias para la vida de Miguel de Cervantes Saavedra*. Several references to his own forthcoming edition are very subtly inserted. There is a statement of his concept of *Don Quixote:* "I have for many years past regarded *La historia de Don Quixote de La Mancha* as a classic, and have nearly completed an edition of it as such...." [2] Bowle's interest in Cervantes' novel and in Spanish literature in general had developed over a long period of years. The edition of *Don*

---

[1] *The Dictionary of National Biography,* II (London, 1921-1922), p. 974.
[2] John Bowle, letter to the editor of the *Gentleman's Magazine,* LI (1781), p. 22.

Quixote is only the culmination of his endeavors in the Romance languages. He had earlier been making investigations of other works and had brought forth noteworthy and little-known facts.

Checking in a publication of the time, *Archaeologia*, I found several articles by Bowle on diverse topics. For example, in Volume VII, page 214, he writes about musical instruments referred to in *Le Roman De La Rose*. Volume VIII of the same magazine has two articles, both of which later have some connection with the edition of *Don Quixote*. The first article (which starts on page sixty-seven) concerns parish registers, and the second deals with playing cards. Herein Bowle mentions the origin of games in Spain called *veintiún* and *quince:* "we are indebted to the same quarter [Spain] for another, yet sometime used, and that is the *Veyntun*. *Cervantes* in his pleasing Novel of Rinconete y Cortadillo, makes the former of these sharpers acquaint his comrade that he had got his livelihood betwixt Madrid and Sevil by this game — *jugando a la veyntiuna* . . . . From the same source we have the Quinze." [3]

One is a little astonished to realize how far-reaching Bowle's acquaintance with Spanish customs is when he refers us to a place in the *Anotaciones a Don Quixote* where he has a note on this same subject. In the *Anotaciones* he supplies an explanation from Covarrubias to clarify what Cervantes meant when he wrote "perder por carta de más, que de menos" (*Don Quixote*, Part II, chapter 17): "Pecar por *carta* de mas, ó por carta de menos, quando, ó se excede, ó no se llegó al justo. Es tomado del juego del Quinze, ó del veinte y uno. Cov." [4]

To discover more about the editor, I continued to use this method of closely examining all the articles and letters I could find. I was soon aware that Bowle had been making other literary investigations of some significance before beginning in earnest on his edition of *Don Quixote*. For instance, in the 1750's he

---

[3] Bowle, "Observations on Card Playing," *Archaeologia*, VIII (London, 1787), p. 151. To avoid bewilderment on the reader's part, it should be noted here at the outset that all quotations are exact. For this reason, unexpected underlining and lack of capitals exist, especially in the quotations from Bowle.

[4] Bowle, *Anotaciones a Don Quixote, Segunda Parte,* in his edition of *Don Quixote*, III (London, 1781), p. 48.

had detected William Lauder's forgeries concerning John Milton. [5] In 1765 he had published miscellaneous pieces of English poetry, containing Shakespeare's *King John* and some of the satires of Marston. [6]

In the 1770's he had begun contributing to the works of various contemporaries. He made numerous suggestions to James Granger for his *A Biographical History of England*. In a long letter dated October 1, 1772, he gave Granger "a few other particulars, which I hope will be worth your notice." [7] It contains notes on various Spaniards who had visited England and whom he deemed worthy of more attention in Granger's work. The comments about Pedro de Rivadeneyra (whose *Vida de San Ignacio* is referred to often in the *Anotaciones*) deserve attention because they give us an insight into the character and mind of Bowle himself:

> I shall begin with Ribadeneyra, who came hither [England], as he himself informs us, with the Duke de Feria, towards the end of the year 1588. I wish there was any print of him, to entitle him to a place in your work; as, though he is partial enough to his own religion, there is less acrimony and rancour in his account of our schism, as he stiles it, than in the writings of the Italians, Pollini and Davanzati, on the same subject; and his work abounds in curious anecdotes respecting the personal character of Queen Mary. But his life of Loyola is most for our present purpose. [8]

---

[5] In early 1747 Lauder published an article in the *Gentleman's Magazine* saying that Milton was a plagiarist, and finally in 1750, he published "An Essay on Milton's Use and Imitation of the Moderns in his *Paradise Lost*." Richard Richardson began questioning the veracity of Lauder's statements while Samuel Johnson defended Lauder in the ensuing arguments. Bowle first detected the fraud, and was supported in his belief when John Douglas, afterwards Bishop of Salisbury, came independently to the conclusion that Lauder's assertions were false. Lauder was disgraced, and involved Johnson in some embarrassment from which, however, the latter's integrity and honesty saved him. (*Dictionary of National Biography*, XI, p. 642).

[6] *Ibid.*, II, p. 974.

[7] Rev. James Granger, *Letters Between the Rev. James Granger, M.A. Rector of Shiplake, and Many of the Most Eminent Literary Men of his Time* (London, 1805), p. 37.

[8] *Ibid.*, pp. 37-38.

Although I am not sure that Bowle was inherently a tolerant or patient man, his comments on the restraint of Rivadeneyra plus the insight he has into this man, both here and elsewhere, indicate that the editor could accept others as they were. In his indirect praise of Rivadeneyra, we also notice a love for Spain and her writers. At all times he is respectful of Spanish authors, and in his study of Cervantes, this respect reaches its highest degree. It is as if he saw in Spain a wealth of artistic genius not fully realized by his contemporaries. This awareness grows as we see him progress from such tame statements about Rivadeneyra as "though he is partial enough... in his account of our schism..." to some rather lyrical declarations about Cervantes a few years later.

Bowle's remarks about the early progress of his edition are enlightening. In them he becomes more forthright about the time and research he had put into his work. The boldness with which he writes increases as his letters become more frequent. The most helpful and most numerous statements about his edition are contained in letters to Dr. Thomas Percy, Bishop of Dromore, who was already well-known for his *Reliques of Ancient English Poetry*. In 1777 Bowle addressed two letters to Dr. Percy which indicate that he was progressing at a good pace with his proposed edition. (In this same year Bowle also published a letter, actually a book, to Dr. Percy. In it he presented the public his plans for his edition of *Don Quixote*.) From London on May 11, he sent Dr. Percy some notes on Shakespeare. In the letter he mentions being "embarked in a weighty business," [9] and one may assume that he is referring to his *Anotaciones a Don Quixote*, of which he hopes to give Dr. Percy the first copy.

In another letter to Dr. Percy in October he speaks of having read *El verdadero suceso de la famosa batalla de Roncesvalles, con la muerte de los doze pares de Francia*. The reference to this book gives him the opportunity of speaking of his own project. He first mentions a letter from Don Casimiro de Ortega to a

---

[9] John Nichols, *Ilustrations of the Literary History of the Eighteenth Century*, VIII (London, 1831), p. 166.

Mr. Ventades [10] in which the *Don-Quixote* project is greatly lauded. The individuals mentioned by Bowle are quickly dismissed, and the letter is used as a springboard to write more exuberantly than ever about his plans for the edition of *Don Quixote* and the general reception which they have had so far:

> I have lately had some friendly hints... through Mr. White, though he did not acquaint me from whom they came. But a letter to him from Rome, of the first instant, from John Talbot Dillon, Esq. promises great things. The writer says that, having lived many years in his youth in Spain, he acquired a most perfect knowledge of the language; that he has by him a very large collection of notes, critical and historical, with Illustrations of Don Quixote, explaining all the hard words and difficult passages, the whole being the result of near twenty years' study, and two journeys into Spain and Portugal; and desires to know if the same would be agreeable to him or the ingenious author in question. I have answered his letter, and thanking him for his offer, have closed with his proposal, giving him an abstract of what I have done, inclosing my proposals and map, and hope to hear further from him when I come to town [London], which most probable [sic] will be very early December. [11]

The John Dillon whom he cites here with such enthusiasm was a Baron of the Holy Roman Empire. He was recognized at the time for his knowledge of the Iberian Peninsula, having written a work entitled *Travels Through Spain*. In the prologue to the *Anotaciones* Bowle speaks of him with the same fervor, leading one to believe that our editor tended toward exaggeration in his relationships with others, especially in literary and

---

[10] Casimiro de Ortega, a royal professor of botany at Madrid, is praised in Dillon's *Travels Through Spain:* "The ingenious and learned Dr. Ortega was in England a few years ago, and is well known to several gentlemen in this country." (p. 91).

John Crookshanks (to be mentioned later in this chapter) in a letter (now in the manuscript collections of the British Museum Library) to Bowle in April, 1776, mentions this Mr. Ventades: "I was just now to call on Mr. Ventades the Spanish Consul, to read him your last Letter, by way of making a little court, & to invite him to dine with me, to meet you either the 24 or 25."

[11] Nichols, pp. 169-170.

commercial ones: "Pero me considero por muy dichoso en aver alcanzado la Noticia y Atencion del Señor D. JUAN TALBOT DILLON, Baron y Cavallero del sacro Romano Imperio, que, desde Roma en el mes de Octubre de 1777 me favoreció primeramente con su correspondencia." [12]

In a letter from the Baron Dillon to Dr. Percy not long after the appearance of the edition of *Don Quixote* in 1781, Dillon again refers to Bowle as that "ingenious editor" who "has done me more honour than I deserve." [13] However, one senses a certain restraint on the part of the writer throughout the letter (only the first part of which directly concerns Bowle). He delivers a mild criticism about the edition also, and his attitude is very much in contrast to that bubbling one found in Bowle's letter and prologue.

In Nichols' *Literary Anecdotes* there is a series of letters between a Rev. Michael Tyson and a Mr. Richard Gough. In January, 1780, Tyson writes: "Is Bowle's Don Quixote published or not? Though I did not chuse to seem to be acquainted with the Editor by appearing amongst the Subscribers, yet I like Cervantes so much, that I must make a swap, or truck, with Tom Payne for the book." [14]

One wonders why he did not "chuse" to be associated with the editor. Was there some kind of personal disagreement between them? We are at a loss to explain the attitude here except that Gough in a return letter in April, 1780, makes an innocent statement which may be some reason for Tyson's behavior. Speaking of a gathering of gentlemen one evening, he says: "Everything was conducted with the strictest decorum. Bowle was uncommonly well behaved...." [15]

To Gough at least, and probably to Tyson, Bowle was not the quietest individual around or the most pleasant to get along with. Unfortunately, we have none of Bowle's statements to answer or contradict any of these specific quotations. Yet it is evident that Bowle had a straightforward manner which might

---

[12] Bowle, *Anotaciones*, Prólogo, III, p. xi.
[13] Nichols, p. 193.
[14] Nichols, *Literary Anecdotes of the Eighteenth Century*, VIII (London, 1812), p. 660.
[15] *Ibid.*, p. 667.

cause hard feelings. Such an attitude could also easily involve its possessor in many difficulties. And difficulties are exactly what began occurring in 1781. As the publication date of his work drew near, Bowle became much more self-assertive. As a result he made himself an ideal target for criticism. The publication of the edition of *Don Quixote* was met with some unfriendly criticism, and this, naturally, was unpalatable to the editor. In addition to his literary troubles, there were domestic occurrences which also embittered his outlook on life. While searching through Nichols' *Illustrations* for material pertaining to Bowle, I came across one very poignant paragraph in a letter from a Mr. J. C. Brooks to Mr. Gough. This was written in December of 1782: "Bowle called upon me a day or two ago, and is much broken. His nephew, a young man who married his only daughter, died last summer, to the great affliction of all the family. A John Bowle, his grandson, is now almost his sole joy...."[16]

In Bowle it is easy to picture a naturally eager and energetic man who has spent his life in pursuit of knowledge. He is a man who has accumulated reams of data on a wide field of subjects, and who, finally in his full maturity, has brought forth the fruits of his labors in carefully produced tomes. He expects that now, with all his great investigative work publicly displayed, he can sit back and listen to the praise which he thinks should be his. Instead, his work receives little of the acclaim its author expects. Not only does he suffer this humiliation; he is roundly attacked by one of the most vitriolic critics of the time. He must suffer this public embarrassment while undergoing a more private grief within his family. There can be no wonder at all at the openly angry attacks which Bowle begins to direct at his critics in 1784. Understanding his personality, and the situations which have molded this personality to a certain degree, one can feel only a deep sympathy for him at this time.

In a letter to the *Gentleman's Magazine* dated August, 1784, Bowle speaks out against his adversaries, who have evidently become more vociferous since 1781. To oppose their negative statements, he inserts portions of a letter from a favorable reader

---

[16] Nichols, *Illustrations*, VI, p. 411.

of his edition. But the main purpose of the letter is to complain about the way his edition has been refused reviews by certain journals:

> As I have within a few days past discovered some very unfair practices respecting the admission of an account of my edition of Don Quixote into two periodical publications, to which I had some reason to think I was entitled, and have found the perpetrators of them to have been a false friend, and another, whose encomium I should regard as an affront and real slander... I beg leave, in justice to myself, to request of you to insert the following extract from a letter, which I received last month.... [17]

By 1785 he can no longer stand the abuse (real and imagined) to which he has fallen victim. In this year he writes four letters to the *Gentleman's Magazine*. Each one becomes progressively more bitter and more cutting. They are of interest because they show how Bowle hits back at his attackers (here they are all against one man, Giuseppe Baretti). Underneath, they reveal our editor much more than he was ever aware or most certainly he would never have written them as he did. None of them is signed with his own name but rather they carry the signature or initials of some improbable individual. Many other letters in this periodical are signed in the same way. However, in all of his earlier, eager letters Bowle signed his own name. It is as if now, even though very angry and properly self-righteous, he were afraid to make himself known with his former exuberance.

In the first of these letters (July, 1785) signed *Querist*, he begins talking about Samuel Johnson (whose recent death had occasioned numerous letters at the time to the *Gentleman's Magazine* — thus making Bowle's letter sound all the more innocent). He criticizes Johnson for having been "apologist for two culprits arraigned for atrocious offences at the bar of justice, viz. Messieurs Savage and Baretti." He lunges out at Baretti by condemning Johnson's testimony which, if it was as weak as Bowle

---

[17] Bowle, letter to the editor of the *Gentleman's Magazine*, LIV (1784, II), pp. 565-566.

presents it, is rather ludicrous: " 'Mr. Baretti, says he [Johnson], is a man of letters, and a studious man; he never picks up prostitutes in the street, that I know of; he is short-sighted, and so am I; and, I believe, would not assault a man without provocation.' " [18]

Bowle's next letter, signed *Anti-Janus*, appears in August, 1785, and is openly directed against Baretti. Giuseppe Baretti was a well-known writer, traveler, and literary critic, who lived in England for some time and was a friend of Samuel Johnson. It seems to have been Baretti's misfortune or delight (I am not sure which) to have stirred up acrimonious controversies. Many of his published letters are nothing more than diatribes against his contemporaries; and yet, while making many lasting enemies, he won the praise and general approval of the leading men of his time. Among his articles are letters on England and Englishmen. Here in his own letter Bowle decries the earlier acclaim Baretti received while in England. He says that Baretti called London the

> "sink of Europe...." It is some years since I read those letters, and therefore do not remember many particulars; but, upon the whole, I do aver, that he has represented England, and London in particular, not as it really is, or then was, but as he wished it to be. It was, however, in this sink of Europe, where he stabbed a man to death, and where he was tried and acquitted of murder. [19]

In his next letter of September, 1785, signed simply X. Y., Bowle refers to his first letter in July. He retracts some of the underlying criticism of Johnson in that letter. Evidently he realizes how foolish he actually sounded and attempts to excuse some of his unnecessary censure of Johnson. Besides in part rectifying his uncalled-for attitude in the first letter, this letter has an amusing charm provided by the author's shrewdness. Bowle does not mention Baretti here at all. By referring back some one-hundred pages, he slyly makes the reader look back in the magazine to see what has been going on: "In extenuation of

---

[18] Bowle, letter to the editor of the *Gentleman's Magazine*, LV (1785, II), p. 497.
[19] *Ibid.*, p. 608.

Dr. Johnson's foibles respecting two of the culprits, p. 497, it may be urged, that though he had been long acquainted with the second [Baretti], he did not discover the man till very late." [20]

Finally in October his last letter in this group appears. It too has only initials for a signature: *J. C.* Bowle goes all out in his condemnation and calles Baretti "sly, petulant, impudent, a slanderer and flatterer, a bully and poltroon, dissolute, fool, and, in short, adorned with every abominable endowment." Again he refers to his previous articles as if other individuals had written them. He does not specifically mention Baretti, but his naming the subject's productions can leave no doubt as to who is the object of his scorn. Bowle returns to a little of his old exuberance at the end of the letter and announces a new book that has come out in which one can see exactly the "great worth and learning" of Baretti. [21] He also mentions that the book or pamphlet has received notice in the last *Monthly Review*. A check here shows the reviewer impartial and somewhat bewildered by the quarrel which has been growing for four years and now becomes public. [22] This mysterious booklet by Bowle is called *Remarks on the Extraordinary Conduct of the Knight of the Ten Stars and his Italian Esquire, to the Editor of Don Quixote: in a Letter to the Rev. J.S.D.D.*

The identity of the Rev. J.S.D.D., to whom the book is addressed, is never made clear. [23] Bowle's name does not appear in the book anywhere, and we would be almost inclined to doubt

---

[20] *Ibid.*, p. 675.
[21] *Ibid.*, p. 760.
[22] *The Monthly Review*, LXXIII (London, 1786), p. 156: "We acknowledge ourselves incompetent judges, as to the real grounds of the dispute or quarrel, which has given rise to these strictures. If Mr. Bowle, to whom the Public hath lately been obliged for a valuable edition of Don Quixote, in the original Spanish, hath been ill-treated by Signior [sic] Baretti, or others, he hath here, we apprehend, amply avenged himself on his adversary's character and writings."
[23] A rather dubious clarification is given in the nineteenth century by one J. H. Burn, who sold the Crookshanks-Bowle correspondence between 1774-1777 to the British Museum Library (manuscript collections). Mr. Burn says in a note to a letter from 1774: "The 'Mr. Smith,' mentioned in the first, dated July 14, 1774, is in later letters noticed as 'Dr. Smith.' He is evidently the same party noticed in the following — Remarks on the extraordinary conduct of the knight of the Ten Stars...."

that the editor himself wrote it except that his initials are at the end along with the date of January, 1785. The principal recipient of the attack in the beginning is the "Knight of the Ten Stars," who is referred to merely as don Juan C**********. Then after a few pages, the assault is directed toward his "Italian Esquire," who, we soon discover, is Baretti. From here on, Bowle leaves aside his rather formal manner used in speaking of the "Knight" and devotes all his energies to tearing Baretti apart, referring to him rather derogatively as *Baretti* or *B*.

The bitterness which is all too apparent in this booklet has a somewhat involved origin and development. It goes back to the time just before the publication of Bowle's edition of *Don Quixote* and to the years following. During the time he was writing his edition, Bowle wrote frequently to his friends about his project and how it was progressing. We have seen how he wrote most enthusiastically to Dr. Percy and to the *Gentleman's Magazine* about his plans. For some reason, he failed to thank some people publicly for their help, and among those omitted was a certain John Crookshanks. From what Bowle says in his remarks, his contacts with this old gentleman were quite friendly.[24] When Bowle wrote the prologue to his *Anotaciones* and showed it to Crookshanks, the latter was not at all pleased with it, however. Since we are only indirectly told what the reason was for his displeasure, we assume that Crookshanks was not happy with the way his help had been seemingly overlooked.

At the end of the *Remarks,* Bowle summarizes his own feelings:

> I am engaged in a disagreeable undertaking [the writing of the *Remarks*]; but am forced to it from the necessity of self-defence, in opposition to the grossest deception; high conceit, self-sufficiency, and real ignorance. This is not all: I may also add, evil speaking, slander, and much uncharitableness; a heavy charge; which I am sorry to say, is but too-well founded, and which I know to be true.

---

[24] The Crookshanks-Bowle correspondence between 1774 and 1777 supports such a statement, for Crookshanks writes on June 6, 1776: "I wait with impatience to hear from you & have only to repeat, do not spare me, when & where I can contribute to your satisfaction pleasure & Profit in bringing forward your design."

I will trouble you [the Rev. J.S.] with an extract from my last letter, to the principal in this business [the Knight of the Ten Stars, Crookshanks]. 'What a man must I have been, after your many professions, after acquainting you with my progress, and accidental lucky discoveries, if it could have entered into my thoughts, that you was [sic] treasuring up a load of concealed malevolence, to be discharged against me at a certain season, when there was a prospect of doing me essential injury? I should loath and detest myself, if such had been the frame of my mind.' The case stands thus: I had experienced at his hands several acts of apparent generosity; which, I am conscious, I ever studied, to the utmost of my abilities, to return; by openly communicating my whole plan, as I went along; and, as far as in me lay, gratifying him in his pursuits, whenever occasion offered. But having, inadvertently, omitted all complements [sic] to *his talents*, by a total silence of his name; and observed, in my Letter to Dr. Percy, *Baretti's* egregiously defective and erroneous account of Spanish Literature... that they should unite their forces against me, may be readily admitted. [25]

The quarrel could have been patched up between the two former friends perhaps if it had not been for the intrusion of a third party. The individual who caused the argument to become more vitriolic was Giuseppe Baretti. We find that while Baretti was living in England for a period of time, Bowle's edition of *Don Quixote* was published. Before 1781 he had not known Bowle well. The enmity in its initial stages was not of an inherently personal sort, therefore, for it began in a rather innocent manner.

In 1781 Baretti was tutoring two young friends of Crookshanks in Spanish. He was already a close friend of this gentleman (who before 1781 was still a friend of Bowle). To see the Spanish language at its best, he decided to use a copy of *Don Quixote*, and wanting to have the most recent edition available, he borrowed a copy of Bowle's edition from Crookshanks. As was his custom, Baretti inserted notes in the margins where he found errors or

---

[25] Bowle, *Remarks on the Extraordinary Conduct of the Knight of the Ten Stars*... (London, 1785), pp. 40-41.

statements with which he was in disagreement. When Bowle was made aware of these notations plus some adverse criticisms by the Italian, he was immediately incensed. Baretti's actions, along with Crookshanks' unfavorable criticism, stirred Bowle to rash statements, and from here on the polemic grew and grew. Baretti was the individual chiefly responsible for the cold reception of Bowle's edition. It was he who asserted enough influence for it to be treated, if at all by the reviewers, with more indifference than warmth.

Baretti lost no time in replying to Bowle's *Remarks,* and within a few months his own pamphlet entitled *Tolondron* appeared. It is a series of speeches which are quite sarcastic, but, because of Baretti's inherent humor, they are very entertaining. His statements have much validity, but he lets his sarcasm and "cuteness" overtake his good sense entirely too often. Near the end of the book he delivers the following comments which are a good summary of his general attitude toward Bowle and his edition of *Don Quixote:*

> But, to be serious, if it is possible to be serious when about so merry a subject ... Don Quixote is a book that wants no *Comento,* but what may be contained in two or three pages, as very few are the things in it that want explanation and clarification.... Far from harbouring any such idea or hinting, that to understand his Don Quixote, we were to read the chivalry and other silly books he had read himself, Cervantes condemned them all to be burnt by means of the Curate.... Fling you, Mr. John Bowle, fling into the fire your *Comento* likewise; as I tell it you again, that there is not *one line* throughout Don Quixote in want of any of your explanations....[26]

It is with this note of extreme bitterness and personal enmity that the clash between Bowle and Baretti reaches a climax in 1785. If the quarrel were merely one which affected two rather hot-headed individuals and nothing else, we could laugh at the whole matter. Unfortunately, because the polemic is raised by Bowle's edition of *Don Quixote,* the conflict has results which

---

[26] Giuseppe Baretti, *Tolondron* (London, 1786), pp. 308-310.

involve far more than these two men. Baretti's too vehement criticism of Bowle initially prevents a general acceptance of the edition as a valid contribution to Cervantean scholarship. The Italian's rejection of Bowle's work is taken up by other scholars, and Bowle's edition is considered, at best, an interesting potpourri of facts about Cervantes and *Don Quixote*. The scholars who do study the edition do not hesitate to use any pertinent material they find, however — usually without citing the source. Bowle and his edition are placed in an ironic, if not paradoxical, situation, therefore: he, the first editor of *Don Quixote*, and his commentary are hastily overlooked, or forgotten, in the development of truly modern Cervantean investigations — investigations which begin precisely with John Bowle.

II

DON QUIXOTE IN THE SEVENTEENTH AND EIGHTEENTH CENTURIES

Bowle's edition of *Don Quixote* appears some one hundred and seventy years after the novel's first publication in Spain. In these years there are many publications of the novel, and there are new ideas advanced about it. In order to fit Bowle's edition properly into the development of Cervantean criticism, in this chapter we shall view the attitudes concerning *Don Quixote* and Cervantes through the end of the eighteenth century.

It is widely believed that *Don Quixote* was an immediate success in Spain. However, it is also proposed that the novel and its author were greatly criticized. But neither acclaim nor censure adequately describes the situation. The modern critics should be saying that more than anything else *surprise* was expressed — surprise as the public gradually realized the newness and uniqueness of the work. The question of why Don Quixote became so much a household figure has been discussed over and over, especially during our own century. Was it merely because of the work's humor and laughing satire (which are the usual reasons given) or was there really a more profound appeal that the public found in it?

In the seventeenth century we find the people reading *Don Quixote* mainly to be entertained. People see the knight and his squire as two misguided bumpkins caught up in a maze of adventures brought on by the knight's foolhardiness. In addition they interpret in the wild actions of the principal protagonists an avid desire on the part of Cervantes to ridicule the books of chivalry. From here they go a bit further to declare that the author is ridiculing all aspects of society which are out of step and exaggerated. Beyond this somewhat artificial view of *Don Quixote,* there is no more probing into the work and what it is about.

Guided by this superficial interpretation of *Don Quixote,* several imitations appear during the first hundred years of the novel's existence. These are not many in number nor are they very important, but, just as the references to be mentioned below, they are helpful in understanding the growing popularity of *Don Quixote* in seventeenth-century Spain. Among the more noteworthy writers attracted by the novel was Quevedo, who wrote a mocking *Testamento de Don Quixote* in 1608. Guillén de Castro wrote a *Comedia del curioso impertinente,* and about 1620 he published a play entitled *Don Quixote de la Mancha.*[1] It concerns the episode of Dorotea, Don Fernando, Luscinda, and Cardenio. Juan de Burgos composed a "romance a lo gracioso" in 1657, concerning Sancho's complaints to Don Quixote about his perpetual state of hunger.

There are numerous references to *Don Quixote* in works of the seventeenth century, and the playwrights are the ones who mention the work most often. The novel obviously had to be well known by the public, for otherwise the dramatist would have been criticized and laughed at for citing something unfamiliar to his audience. One can be sure no writer would have willingly courted disapproval. Calderón's *El alcalde de Zalamea* refers specifically to *Don Quixote.* If the playwright was willing to cite the novel in the 1640's, he must have thought that the book was sufficiently popular to merit such acknowledgment. One of his references is enough for us to see how familiar *Don Quixote* had become to an audience of the mid-seventeenth century. (The captain and sergeant, having just arrived in Zalamea a while before, comment on two figures approaching:)

CAPITÁN: ... Mas ¿qué ruido es ése?
SARGENTO: Un hombre
que de un flaco rocinante

---

[1] The Hispanic Society of America has a copy published in Valencia in 1905 giving an historical account of the play.

> a la vuelta desa esquina
> se apeó, y en rostro y talle
> parece aquel Don Quijote,
> de quien Miguel de Cervantes
> escribió las aventuras. ²

Tirso in his *El castigo del penséque* has the following citation which indicates an even wider acquaintance by the public with Cervantes' works as a whole.

> DON RODRIGO: ¿Hay sucesos semejantes?
> CHINCHILLA: Cuando los llegue a saber
> Madrid, los ha de poner
> en sus novelas Cervantes. ³

Indirectly from these and from other similar remarks, we get the impression that Don Quixote was merely a ridiculous figure. In general, therefore, the seventeenth-century individual essentially thought that the hero was created to ridicule favorite chivalric protagonists who engaged in wild, temerarious escapades. ⁴

Yet, while Cervantes was poking fun at the chivalric books, he was doing it in a very special way. For in *Don Quixote*, the protagonist is not really absurd in the sense of being unbelievable (as is the degenerated figure of Roland in *Orlando furioso*). Cervantes imagined a man of flesh and blood — Don Quixote is drawn from real life; he is Quijano el bueno. From this fact comes the eventual realization of the symbolism, inherent in Don Quixote, of the clash between reality and dream. It is during the eighteenth century that we find this idea first occurring. From approximately 1720 on, we may say that two views concerning *Don Quixote* exist in Spain: the old idea of *Don Quixote's* being a superficial work for amusement and a new one which very slowly grows, timidly hinting that there may be something of greater value lying beneath the surface of the adventures of the knight and his squire.

---

² Pedro Calderón de la Barca, *El alcalde de Zalamea* (Madrid, 1961), pp. 15-16.
³ Gabriel Téllez, *Comedias escogidas de Fray Gabriel Téllez* (Madrid, 1850), p. 74.
⁴ For some interesting thoughts on this subject the reader should consult Herrero García's *Estimaciones literarias del siglo XVII*.

Two writers show best the first side of the Spanish eighteenth-century view toward Cervantes and, more specifically, toward *Don Quixote*. Professor Sebold in his edition of Padre Isla's novel makes some observations concerning the genesis and background of *Fray Gerundio*. He finds in the protagonist a joining of the characteristics of the *pícaro* and Don Quixote. In essence, Isla sees only those picaresque elements in *Don Quixote* which he wants to see and then incorporates them into *Fray Gerundio* ("... se conoce a los demás rústicos — parientes de Gerundico — por rasgos cada vez más ridículos y repulsivos. A tales detalles y a alguna descripción, a la que se une lo picaresco, se reduce lo patentemente cervantino en el Gerundio.").[5] Sebold then goes on to show that another writer is very similar in the attitude he exhibits toward Don Quixote. One Nicolás de Molani Nogui Interiano (probably Torres Villarroel) describes Don Quixote in the most repulsive terms possible: "El cuerpo parecía alma de vizcaíno .... cabellos, por lo grasientos, almibarados, sobre cascos de arrope ... miserable de palabras, avaro de discursos, y hambriento de carnes; la voz entre serpentón, y rebuzno, que parecía, en lo áspero, y bronco, que merendaba Hidalgos y Suegras ...."[6]

In another of his works Isla becomes even more explicit in his concept of the Cervantean hero. The work is *La juventud triunfante* included in *La mojiganga teológica* where Isla describes a student festival. The author makes a comparison between Don Quixote and Capricho: "No era solo este Capricho el que iba en la *Mojiganga;* otro marchaba junto à él, que aunque se llamaba Don Quixote, ya saben los eruditos que *quixote*, y capricho son términos sinónimos, o una misma cosa con nombres diferentes."[7] *Capricho* is pictured as extravagant in dress and becomes actually a symbol of extravagance in all things. In addition, he is a close friend of *Mal Gusto* — hardly a flattering comparison for Don

---

[5] José Francisco de Isla, *Fray Gerundio de Campazas* (Introducción y notas de Russell P. Sebold), I (Madrid, 1960), p. lxiv.

[6] [Diego de Torres Villarroel] Nicolás de Molani Nogui Interiano [pseud.], *Qverella Que Don Quixote De La Mancha Da En El Tribunal De La Mverte Contra Don Francisco De Quevedo*... (Madrid, [n. d.]), pp. 17-18.

[7] Isla, *La mojiganga teológica* (Madrid, 1930), p. 93.

Quixote. Some further remarks by Sebold provide a good summary of the attitudes expressed: "Para Torres Villarroel e Isla, estos detalles [repugnantes, escatológicos] debían parecer tan característicos del *Quijote* como lo son de la novela picaresca asquerosas aventuras como la de Guzmán con la esposa del cocinero .... En fin, viene a ser dudoso qué rasgos fueron para Isla picarescos, y cuáles cervantinos." [8]

From these selections Don Quixote seems much more a detestable figure than a humorous one. These two authors have censured him mercilessly. Yet their opinions are derived precisely from the old seventeenth-century view of the protagonist — that of a doddering fool who satirizes in himself the foibles of his fellow man and his ideals. Don Quixote provokes laughter — but in a way which leads easily to cruelty and malice. Both Isla and Torres have merely carried this earlier idea to an extreme.

This is only one side of the picture, however. During the same general period, Cadalso is writing in his *Cartas marruecas* a very important comment:

> En esta nación hay un libro muy aplaudido por todas las demás. Lo he leído, y me ha gustado sin duda pero no deja de mortificarme la sospecha de que el sentido literal es uno, y el verdadero es otro muy diferente. Ninguna obra necesita más que ésta del diccionario de Nuño. Lo que se lee es una serie de extravagancias de un loco, que cree que hay gigantes, encantadores, etcétera, algunas sentencias en boca de un necio, y con muchas escenas de la vida bien criticadas; pero lo que hay debajo de esta apariencia es, en mi concepto, un conjunto de materias profundas e importantes. [9]

In this quotation there is still inherent, as in all writers of the time, the idea of Don Quixote as a crazy fool. Cadalso does not reject this idea at all. For the first time in Spain, however, we see a slight doubting as to whether there is not more beneath the surface of the work. Cadalso is significant in the history of Cervantean interpretation for first suggesting more profundity in the *Quixote*. It is for this reason that we cannot blindly accept the

---

[8] Isla, *Fray Gerundio de Campazas*, I, p. lxvi.
[9] José Cadalso, *Cartas marruecas* (Buenos Aires, 1952), pp. 108-109.

opinions of Isla and Torres Villarroel given above as wholly representative of the Spanish view toward *Don Quixote* in the eighteenth century. They represent only one segment of the criticism of the period, for by the last quarter of the century new concepts are slowly emerging which affect consideration of *Don Quixote* for the next two hundred years.

A change of attitude toward the work is evidenced in one other way also. The most outstanding achievement of the eighteenth century concerning Cervantes is the production of learned volumes about him and his work. The first of these is a life of Cervantes by Don Gregorio Mayáns y Siscar. It was first published in Spain in 1737 (Briga-Real), and then appeared in Tonson's great London edition of *Don Quixote* sponsored in 1738 by John Lord Carteret, Lord Lieutenant of the Kingdom of Ireland.

From a biographical standpoint as well as a critical one, Mayáns' work becomes the point of departure in a new direction of Cervantean investigations. The important opinions on *Don Quixote* in the eighteenth century find their basis here. Through Mayáns' endeavors, a greater interest is awakened in the Spanish novelist. By 1775 Cervantes finally receives a comfortable position in the esteem of his countrymen. In 1778 Pellicer's *Noticias para la vida de Miguel de Cervantes* appears in *Ensayo de una biblioteca de traductores españoles*. Pellicer amplifies what Mayáns said and tries to be more specific in details.

There is an elaborate edition of *Don Quixote* by the Royal Academy in 1780. This is the one containing Vicente de los Ríos' well-known *Análisis del Quixote,* which comes some forty years after Mayáns' investigations. Ríos has the advantage of having at his disposal the investigative efforts of others since 1737. Significantly, he continues Mayáns' comparison of *Don Quixote* to Homeric works.

Several editions appear in the very last years of the century. One is in five volumes containing annotations by Pellicer and carries the dates 1797-1798. Also in these same years an edition of six volumes comes out containing a new résumé of Cervantes' life and work by Manuel José Quintana. Quintana's essay is a complete renovation of the rhetorical and neo-classic critique of a few years earlier. Through him three rather weighty words become popularized: universality, humanity, and originality. He throws aside the artificial and forced parallel between Cervantes and Homer. To him, Cervantes was another Homer, for Cervantes was furnished with his own particular muses and created his novel by means of his own inventive skills. As a result, Quintana maintains that Cervantes is more important and worthy of esteem than the Ancients. [10]

In these last twenty-five years of the eighteenth century, Cervantes' popularity in Spain reaches its first really high crest. The fact that learned editions are published is itself indicative of this new esteem. Even more so are the comments from here and there by other literary figures not directly involved in publishing, editing, or writing critiques of Cervantes' life and works. Among these people is Forner. This man, whose waspish tongue plagued many contemporaries, in his *Oración apologética* places Cervantes above Descartes in merit and satirizes critics who find fault with the novelist. Tomás Antonio Sánchez also protects Cervantes rather spiritedly against attack.

Spain's reaction to *Don Quixote* begins to change somewhat in the eighteenth century, therefore. From the standpoint of critical investigation there is much new interest. As far as judgment of the work goes, we find a continuation of the seventeenth century's superficial interpretation. There is even an exaggerated insistence on this interpretation by Isla and Torres Villarroel. But more significant is the appearance in Cadalso of the first germ of discontent with the old clichés.

In considering *Don Quixote* outside Spain in the seventeenth and eighteenth centuries, we are mainly concerned with France and England. The book is read elsewhere, of course; but, for the purposes of this study, there is little to occupy our attention. An extreme indication of *Don Quixote's* fate in other countries is the first translation of the novel into Portuguese — in 1794. [11] The story of *Don Quixote* in Italy is still incomplete, and what little we know is not too enlightening. In Germany the novel

---

[10] A more complete study of Pellicer and Quintana will be found in the final chapter of this book.

[11] Navarrete (page 465 of his *Vida de Miguel de Cervantes Saavedra*) in the early nineteenth century says that he has seen only one Portuguese translation: *O engenhoso fidalgo Dom Quixote de la Mancha* (Lisbon, 1794 — in six volumes).

comes into its own only from about 1750 on. In the rest of Europe (except for France) and America not very much turns up until practically the beginning of the nineteenth century.

It is France more than England — even more than Spain — that produces the first real beginnings of an interpretation of *Don Quixote*. More editions appear in France than in England during the seventeenth century. As noted in the case of Spain, in France interest is shown principally in the farcical aspect of *Don Quixote*. Up until about 1660 the works of Cervantes are used as sources of theatrical adaptations of all sorts. The most popular parts of his works for such adaptations are not the critical or the satirical, but rather the sentimental and the amorous. Although a translation of Part I of *Don Quixote* is made in 1614 by César Oudin and of Part II in 1618 by François de Rosset (the first translation of *Don Quixote*, Part II, in any language), serious commentary on the novel comes about very slowly.

In the seventeenth century a Frenchman compares Don Quixote to an historical figure. An article in the *Bibliothèque Universelle Et Historique* (tome onzième, 93-140) discusses a book written in English, *The Enthusiasm of the Church of Rome*. It is the first time the relation between Loyola and Don Quixote is made. The anonymous writer says that both were eccentric, extravagant, and too wildly enthusiastic. In the seventeenth and eighteenth centuries, in France especially, this is rather unpopular terminology. It is not until the Romantics that enthusiasm is made respectable and, with it, such a comparison of two of Spain's heroes. Yet the idea is nevertheless expressed years before the Romantic movement.

Pierre Perrault in 1679 writes a *Critique Du Livre de don Quichotte*. The work is mostly negative in viewpoint, for Perrault does not like Spain or Spaniards, and *Don Quixote* becomes a convenient vehicle for his attack on the nation. With Perrault, *Don Quixote* is involved in the Quarrel of the Ancients and the Moderns. In essence, he says that *Don Quixote* is a modern book and one which has a very high type of serious humor.

Most important of all is that this period in France has one figure of literary significance who goes all out in his admiration for *Don Quixote*. This is Charles de Saint-Evremond. With him also the Quarrel of the Ancients and the Moderns is raised. He believes that the novel can be compared favorably to the Classics. He is thus taking the side of the Moderns and is placing Cervantes with others such as Boileau, Corneille, Racine, etc:

> De tous les livres que j'ai jamais lus, Don Quichotte est celui que j'aimerois mieux avoir fait: il n'y en a point, à mon avis, qui puisse contribuer davantage à nous former un bon goût sur toutes choses. J'admire comme dans la bouche du plus grand fou de la terre, Cervantes a trouvé le moyen de se faire connaitre l'homme le plus entendu, et le plus grand connoisseur qui se puisse imaginer. J'admire la diversité de ses caractères, qui sont les plus recherchés du monde pour les especes [sic], et dans leurs especes [sic] les plus naturels. Quevedo paroît un auteur fort ingénieux: mais je l'estime plus d'avoir voulu brûler [sic] tous ses livres quand il lisoit Don Quichotte, que de les avoir su faire. [12]

Saint-Evremond is the first real admirer of Cervantes and *Don Quixote*. Maurice Bardon best states the reason for this by saying that Cervantes and Saint-Evremond are really kindred spirits. The latter is able to find in Cervantes' work his "propre bon sens, spirituel et joyeux, sa propre ironie, piquante et vive ...." [13]

Except for a few incidental appearances here and there in the latter part of the seventeenth century, references to *Don Quixote* fall from a previous apex reached in the period of Louis XIII. It is necessary to mention one work, however — Filleau de Saint-Martin's French version of *Don Quixote* which begins appearing in 1677. The translator does not stick rigidly to the orignal, but adding new material and interpretations of his own, he naturalizes Cervantes' novel once and for all in France. [14]

It is not until the end of Louis XIV's reign and into the Regency that we find *Don Quixote* regaining the truly widespread

---

[12] Maurice Bardon, *"Don Quichotte" En France au XVII et au XVIII siècle 1605-1815*, I (Paris, 1931), p. 298, quoting Saint-Evremond, *Œuvres*, III, pp. 20-21.
[13] *Ibid.*, p. 301.
[14] See his *Avertissement* (*Histoire De L'admirable Don Quixote de la Manche*, I, (Paris, 1681) for his ideas on a translation: "j'ai crû [sic] qu'une Traduction doit toûjours [sic] conserver quelque odeur de son original... ." (p. *4 verso).

interest enjoyed in the first half of the seventeenth century. About 1730 it begins to influence again the production of novels as well as plays. There are two sound reasons for this resurgence of popularity, which are particularly political and historical. First of all, conditions in France about 1700 are nearly the same as those in Spain about 1600: wars on foreign soil and poverty and misery within the country itself. There are wrongs to be righted and the unfortunate to be protected — much as portrayed in the old romances of chivalry and quite specifically in *Don Quixote.* The second reason is a little more concrete and less idealistically sentimental. Very brusquely, it is the War of the Spanish Succession which rekindles the interest in all things Spanish and, consequently, in *Don Quixote.*

At the beginning of the eighteenth century, Lesage produces a translation of *Don Quixote* which is based more on Avellaneda's Part II (1614). Lesage's principal merit, the verve with which he writes, contributes much to the interest in the novel in this period. Lesage is typical of contemporary authors who, caught up in this enthusiastic style, attempt to present the characters of Cervantes for the public's amusement or to criticize the follies of society.

Marivaux writes *Pharsamon (Folies Romanesques)* in 1712. He ridicules all sentimentality, any naïve idealism, and any exaggeration in language or in emotion; and he writes against the false and the extraordinary. His book is a parody of *Don Quixote.* These writers use Don Quixote and Sancho much like puppets, for they wish to provoke laughter through their handling of the two protagonists. Even more far-reaching is the idea that not only are Don Quixote and Sancho deserving of laughter, but Spain as well. The French writers contend that Spain no longer offers a threat in the political sphere and merits only toleration with a benevolent attitude. They mock Spain's strong adherence to Catholicism and the fall of Spain from world power. They see in her all that is disgusting from a century of rampant fanaticism in religion and government, and gleefully seize Don Quixote and Sancho as easy objects for their scorn.

The French *Encyclopédistes* continue the tradition of seeing in Don Quixote the figure of Ignacio de Loyola. Their interest is primarily for amusement: "Ils sont ... trop de leurs temps, pour que, dans leur conception de l'homme idéal, l'instinct, le sentiment, la passion puissent trouver leur juste place à côté de la raison raisonnante et de sa logique démonstrative. L'impulsif, l'opiniâtre, l'entêté don Quichotte est pour eux le type même de l'insensé." [15]

Voltaire makes the same parallel and also likens Charles XII of Sweden to Don Quixote. [16] It is Voltaire, too, who lifts Sancho out of the category of a fool. His assertion is based on Sancho's wise governing of the Island of Barataria. Voltaire's statement sounds greatly reminiscent of the common eighteenth-century glorification of the simple, primitive man. Voltaire points out that Sancho was indeed wise even though he did not know a word of any law code. [17] All of this is interesting because we have much significance being found in Sancho for the first time. He is considered above the sly bumpkin previously portrayed.

In 1774 there appears a very short-lived review. It is mentioned here to show how there is a determined effort by a certain segment of the French public to obtain a more up-to-date portrait of Spain. This is the *Espagne Littéraire, Politique Et Commerçante, Ou Journal Espagnol Et Portugais*. To an extent it succeeds in changing misconceptions about the Iberian Peninsula. It energetically studies important authors of Spain during the sixteenth and seventeenth centuries. Generally speaking it gives an unbiased picture of cultural currents in Spain during the preceding two-hundred years. Even though the magazine lasts only months and accomplishes nothing tangible, it is important. It is a strong indication that at least a small percentage of French critics can see in Spain something other than a backward, laughable, benighted country — all of which *Don Quixote* had been representing. We are seeing indirectly a re-examination of Cervantes' novel.

Jean Baptiste Boyer d'Argens stresses the moral value of *Don Quixote*. For him, Cervantes had to be a genius to be able to combine in the mouth of a madman the most serious and sublime words. The word *sublime* is unusual and new in this regard. It

---

[15] Bardon, II, p. 548.
[16] "cet homme moitié Alexandre, moitié Don Quichotte...." (Letter, May, 1737) (*Œuvres Complètes, Correspondance*, II (Paris, 1880), p. 270.)
[17] "Je ne connais point de meilleur juge que Sancho Panca: cependant il ne savait pas un mot du code de l'île de Barataria." (*Dictionnaire Philosophique*) (*Œuvres Complètes*, I (Paris, 1867), p. 260.)

is rare that in the eighteenth century anyone should consider Don Quixote's utterances worthy of such terminology. Boyer d'Argens is the first to use the word *sublime* in reference to *Don Quixote*.

Jacques Henri Bernardin de Saint-Pierre ranks *Don Quixote* with the Homeric epic, the Gospels, *Pantagruel*, and *Télémaque*. His statement (in reality not unusual for the period, as we have seen) presents the relationship of historical criticism and *Don Quixote* more clearly than ever before. Other writers had commented on Cervantes' being the destroyer of chivalry, but none of them had been certain as to just when the spirit of chivalry supposedly was in its greatest vogue. Bernardin de Saint-Pierre clearly identifies the spirit of chivalry with what he calls the Middle Ages. As a result, we have the first case of the equation which later becomes so popular: Don Quixote essentially represents the Middle Ages, and Cervantes, by implication, is the Modern Man who turns against his previous black period. This concept is at the basis of much criticism in the nineteenth century. At the end of the eighteenth century again we are upon the threshold of all the "deeper" interpretations which are usually said to spring literally out of nowhere.

Bernardin de Saint-Pierre portrays the Medieval Man as one who might have led a happy life under Christianity if it had not been for the domination of tyrants — both political and religious (especially the latter). To this critic, Rabelais and Cervantes appear as liberators, one out to break the hold of the monks, and the other, the hold of chivalry (representative of non-clerical power). These two geniuses held the two tyrannies up to ridicule and the people were reassured.

In a concluding statement to his study of *Don Quixote* in France in the seventeenth and eighteenth centuries, Maurice Bardon writes: "Résumons-nous. Pour les esprits les plus divers, lecteurs, critiques, dramaturges, romanciers, le *Don Quichotte* est avant tout un ouvrage qui divertit, qui efface les rides d'un front soucieux. Ils n'ont point l'idée que ce soit un livre rare, une merveille littéraire. Et ils le restreignent d'habitude à n'être qu'une satire, — l'un des modèles de la satire." [18]

---

[18] Bardon, II, p. 807.

However, we must realize that, although what Bardon says is generally true, there are some exceptions which tend to be forgotten in the more comprehensive view of the period. We have seen the use of *Don Quixote* as an historical parallel. The word *sublime* has occurred in describing the pronouncements of Don Quixote. Cervantes has been placed on a level with Homer, Rabelais, and Fénelon. *Don Quixote* and Cervantes both have advanced beyond the praise of Saint-Evremond, but significantly this special "praise" is not widespread.

We may conclude that France is the country which keeps the book alive in its earliest and most difficult years. It produces the first references to *Don Quixote* as a very notable modern book and it also produces the first real apologist for Cervantes — that is, Saint-Evremond, who bluntly declares it a great work by a great author. But as we turn from France to England we shall find even greater praise — not so much because of historical or social symbolism, however. Rather the praise comes to Cervantes as a supreme artist and to his book as a model for what later becomes the standard modern narrative — the realistic, psychological novel of character.

Don Quixote makes its first appearance in English in 1612. In that year Thomas Shelton publishes his *History of the valorous and wittie Knight-Errant, Don Quixote of the Mancha*. This translation of Part I is the first complete version in any foreign language. Most likely it was written a few years earlier, for Shelton states that it was done for a friend rather than the general public.[19] Perhaps herein lies an excuse for the hurried, careless work exhibited in the translation. The work holds interest not merely for being the first translation, but also because it has a charm and flavor of English in the time of Shakespeare. A translation of Part II is made by Shelton in 1620 along with a new

---

[19] "Mine Honourable Lord: hauing translated some fiue or six yeeres agoe, the Historie of *Don Quixote*, out of the Spanish tongue, into the English, in the space of fortie dayes: being thervnto more than halfe inforced, through the importunie [sic] of a very deare friend, that was desirous to vnderstand the subject: After I had given him once a view thereof, I cast it aside, where it lay long time neglected in a corner, and so little regarded by me, as I neuer once set hand to reuiew or correct the same." (Shelton, *Don Quixote*, I (London?, 1620?), p. ii of the Dedication to the Lord of Walden.)

edition of Part I. Shelton has two more reprintings in the seventeenth century: 1652 and 1675. The only other translation in this period is one by John Phillips.

We often read that *Don Quixote* was immediately popular and that because of such popularity it wielded considerable influence in England. Edwin B. Knowles believes that this notion is very much of a myth: "This paucity of English versions during the first ninety-five years of *Don Quixote's* existence should be borne in mind," he comments, "when one reads overheated statements about the way the book was enthusiastically received in England. There were fourteen editions of translations in France during the same period." [20] The principal service of *Don Quixote* and Cervantes' minor works during this early period is to provide scattered material for dramatists. First is Beaumont and Fletcher's *The Knight of the Burning Pestle* (c. 1611). Originally it was considered a direct and important imitation of *Don Quixote*. Modern criticism believes that it is only slightly related to Cervantes' novel.

The use of individual episodes from the work is very common. Massinger's *The Second Maiden's Voyage* (1611) comes directly from *El curioso impertinente*. About this same time Field's *Amends for Ladies* appears, which borrows ideas to a lesser degree from *El curioso impertinente* or from Massinger's play.

In the year 1613, just one year after the appearance of Shelton's translation, a play was produced at the English court. A general consensus holds that it was an adaptation of the Cardenio story. Entitled *Cardenno,* it was written by Fletcher and possibly, Shakespeare. Unfortunately, it is impossible to be certain whether Shakespeare was a co-author because the play has disappeared. This is truly lamentable since the possibility of linking concretely the two greatest of Spain's and England's literary artists has been

---

[20] Edwin B. Knowles, "Cervantes and English Literature," *Cervantes Across the Centuries* (New York, 1947), p. 268.

(A contrasting statement of E. Allison Peers is of significance here: "... no os sorprenderá oír que el *Quijote* fue recibido en Inglaterra con aclamación inmediata, sin paralelo en ningún otro país...." — "Cervantes en Inglaterra," *Homenaje a Cervantes,* ed. Francisco Sánchez-Castañer, II (Valencia, 1950), p. 271.)

lost forever. Thus, the theory of Shakespeare's collaboration has not been widely accepted.

There is no use of the major characters in *Don Quixote* until about 1630 when D'Avenant's *The Cruel Brother* appears. In this work we find a country gentleman and his farmer-servant bearing great resemblance to our two heroes. Another brief and purely farcical appearance of the two is in Shirley's *The Triumph of Peace* (1634).

In 1654 Edmund Gayton's *Pleasant Notes Upon Don Quixote* is published. It appears in the eighteenth century as *The Festivous Notes on the History and Adventures of the Renowned Don Quixote*. The book is important mainly in that it is a very early commentary on *Don Quixote*. The author has little feeling for Cervantes as a great writer and treats the novel as a series of humorous incidents. These incidents provide Gayton opportunities to joke indecently and sarcastically. He uses Shelton's translation chapter by chapter, selecting passages and "commenting" on them, and he summarizes much of the story in doggerel verse. Typical of his "creative" abilities are the following lines preceding comments on chapter IV of *Don Quixote:*

> Got from the Inne he lost his way almost,
> Yet wonne the title of the Knight o' th' Post:
> The Whipping-post I meane, where John Haldudo
> Did slash his boy (as many Masters do-do)
> Poore *Andrew* it had better been for thee
> Thou'dst ne're been rescued from the killing tree.
> Thou wert repriev'd but to be surer hanged
> Up by the heeles: But *Don* himself was bang'd;
> A shrewd misfortune to our Errant Sir,
> But who can help't? 'twas fortune *de la guerr.* [21]
>
> (*Pleasant Notes* ..., p. 13)

Gayton sees *Don Quixote* as a convenient frame for all kinds of leering, facetious stories. He finds in Don Quixote no ideals — only an amusing old fool who can convey his (Gayton's) rather tasteless tales. This same brusque, superficial attitude is noticed

---

[21] A good discussion of this incident is found in an article by Edward M. Wilson ("Edmund Gayton on Don Quixote, Andrés, and Juan Haldudo," *Comparative Literature*, II (1950), pp. 64-72.)

in his treatment of all the characters. Gayton's approach to *Don Quixote* is really not too different from that of others at this time (we have seen nearly the same thing in Spain and France). It is only that he is a little more cruel in his opinions than are some of his English and foreign contemporaries. [22]

After 1660 the farcical concept of the novel reaches a peak in its favor with the public. Yet at the same time an increasingly serious interest in the work culminates in translations and critical appraisal at the beginning of the new century. The attitudes of people like Gayton give way to the view that Cervantes' novel is truly a great example of serious satire. Instigating the change in attitude are two factors. The return of the Cavaliers from exile in France, where *Don Quixote* was held in great esteem, indirectly causes a new look to be taken at the novel. Also a new work in imitation of Cervantes' appears in 1663. This is Samuel Butler's *Hudibras*. The protagonists of this mock-heroic poem resemble Don Quixote and Sancho more in a superficial way — in their general relationship to each other and in their wanderings. The poem becomes tremendously popular, and the public sees Butler as a kind of English Cervantes. Since they are familiar with Gayton's sarcastic, belittling interpretation, perhaps in welcome relief, readers find in Butler's poem a spirit more like that of the Spanish work.

In the eighteenth century the translating of *Don Quixote* is continued by such diverse individuals as Captain John Stevens and Pierre Motteux, both of whom publish translations in 1700. These two plus Charles Jarvis' translation in 1742 and Smollett's in 1755 comprise the four basic ones of the century.

In the preface to Motteux's translation we find expressed an idea already seen in France. It is thought that Cervantes was so successful in his banishing of the chivalric romances that the morale of the Spanish nobility suffered a dangerous setback. This view enters England first through Rapin's *Réflections Sur La Poétique de ce temps*, which is widely read after the Restoration.

---

[22] The eighteenth-century edition has the following note: "He [Gayton] was a great punster, and his jokes were sometimes low.... It must be confessed, indeed, that he is sometimes indelicate not to say indecent...." (*Festivous Notes*..., p. iv.)

After Motteux, the concept is continued throughout the century, and in the nineteenth century it is expressed most articulately in Byron's famous phrase about Cervantes' having "smiled Spain's chivalry away."

Moving to a less concrete level, we find that the tone of the entire eighteenth-century interpretation of *Don Quixote* in England is found best in John Locke. In a short appendix entitled "Some Thoughts Concerning Reading and Study for a Gentleman" a little before his death in 1704, Locke states that "Reading is for the improvement of the understanding." He proceeds to stock a good library for the proper gentleman of the day. He recommends including Terence, Virgil, Livy, Quintilian, Tully, and Caesar's *Commentaries*. Of modern writers, he lists Boileau's *Traité Du Sublime*, his own *Two Treatises of Government*, Bacon's *Henry VII*, and Mariana's *History of Spain*. There are others in this list of serious books, but these give an idea of what Locke prefers. Of a less severe type he suggests La Rochefoucauld, La Bruyère, Juvenal, and especially Horace. He then discusses another use of reading — that of "diversion and delight":

> Such are poetical writings, especially dramatic, if they may be free from profaneness, obscenity, and what corrupts good manners; for such pitch should not be handled. Of all the books of fiction, I know none that equals "Cervantes's History of Don Quixote" in usefulness, pleasantry, and a constant decorum. And indeed no writings can be pleasant, which have not nature at the bottom, and are not drawn after her copy. [23]

Briefly then, *Don Quixote* is profitable reading; it has wit and charm; and above all it is in good taste. By implication Locke tells us that, being a true picture of nature, the novel is true to life. The correct eighteenth-century man could hardly ask for more in a book. In Locke's proper library there are men who are matter-of-fact and down-to-earth. There is no foolishness about them; they are not likely to inspire any enthusiasms or idealisms — abhorrent to the "correct" attitude of the time. Locke

---

[23] John Locke, *An Essay Concerning Human Understanding*, II (Boston, 1813), pp. 363-369.

in his own way is affirming what we noted in France: that *Don Quixote* is thought to be a first-rate work. For him *Don Quixote* has become a classic.

If any man represents for most people the spirit of constructive eighteenth-century thought in England, it is Samuel Johnson. He concerns us because of his references to both Cervantes and *Don Quixote*. Dr. Thomas Percy tells Boswell for his admirable biography:

> "when a boy he [Johnson] was immoderately fond of reading romances of chivalry, and he retained his fondness for them through life; so that (adds his Lordship) spending part of a summer at my parsonage-house in the country, he chose for regular reading the old Spanish romance of *Felixmarte of Hircania*, in folio, which he read quite through. Yet I have heard him attribute to these extravagant fictions that unsettled turn of mind which prevented him ever fixing in any profession." [24]

(Ticknor adds a facetious statement in his *History of Spanish Literature* to the effect that one may doubt whether any Englishman since Johnson has read the book in its entirety.) [25]

In several places Johson evinces a love and respect for Cervantes and his work. In the *Lives of the Poets* when discussing Samuel Butler he writes: "Cervantes had so much kindness for Don Quixote, that, however he embarrasses him with absurd distresses, he gives him so much sense and virtue as may preserve our esteem: wherever he is, or whatever he does, he is made by matchless dexterity commonly ridiculous, but never contemptible." [26]

Johnson is really not so much interested in the utility or, above all, the morality of the book as is Locke. Johnson basically likes the artistry of *Don Quixote*. For him it is high entertainment, and more, for he sees in Don Quixote and Sancho more universal characteristics. In this way Johnson elevates the two protagonists

---

[24] James Boswell, *The Life of Samuel Johnson*, I (London, 1811), p. 25.
[25] George Ticknor, *History of Spanish Literature*, I (New York, 1854), p. 241.
[26] Samuel Johnson, *Lives of the Poets*, ed. Mrs. Alexander Napier, I (London, 1890), p. 207.

from any subservient role which they have hitherto enjoyed. They no longer serve as the butt of jokes and sarcastic humor. With him they take on the qualities of human individuals who serve as compassionate mirrors of us, the readers and the ordinary men they represent:

> ... very few readers, amidst their mirth or pity, can deny that they have admitted visions of the same kind [like those of Don Quixote]; though they have not, perhaps, expected events equally strange, or by means equally inadequate. When we pity him, we reflect on our own disappointments; and when we laugh, our hearts inform us that he is not more ridiculous than ourselves, except that he tells what we have only thought. [27]

The use of the word *pity* may sound strange coming from Samuel Johnson. He was seemingly such a brusque individual who cared little for the feelings of those around him that this particular word is almost grotesque. However, he was subject to fits of sentimentality and emotion which might well indicate that he was covering up more intimate reactions than his gruff exterior admitted. He, like Cervantes, was direct and to the point in his dislike of sham. The two saw in the latter's creation of Don Quixote a figure who contained much of themselves. In Johnson's case this figure tended most often to lie hidden. It is easier then to understand Johnson's admiration for the novel. In his praise of the work and his declaration of a new quality to be encountered in it, he is early anticipating the more "tender" feelings aroused in the Romantics at the very end of his own century.

In order to consider another aspect of the influence Cervantes has in the same period, we go to Henry Fielding. Fielding's knowledge of *Don Quixote* is quite extensive, but his interpretation of the novel differs little from the superficial one of most of his contemporaries. He does not see the advance in technique and idea in Part II; he always thinks of the potpourri that is Part I — the seemingly chance joining of incidents and ideas. He

---

[27] Samuel Johnson, *The Rambler* (No. 2, 1750), I (London, 1794), pp. 9-10.

does not realize that the framework of a journey has moved from the physical realm in Part I to a more psychological one in Part II.

There are three works of Fielding which show particularly an influence from Cervantes. The first is a play entitled *Don Quixote in England*. It was produced around 1734 with some success. The intention of the play is to satirize corruption in English county politics. Fielding holds to the eighteenth-century idea that in all mankind there is a little of Don Quixote. The use of the characters of *Don Quixote* is about all that concerns us here, for there is little to do really with the Spanish novel other than the names of characters and some superficial similarities in attitude and atmosphere.

Fielding's novel *Joseph Andrews* indicates on the title page that it is written in imitation of Cervantes. Don Quixote is the model for the Rev. Mr. Abraham Adams, especially from the comic angle. Still Fielding does not penetrate the true character of Don Quixote to see that there is something more profound in the Manchegan hero than a mere vehicle for laughter and satire.

In *Tom Jones*, Fielding's approach is again much the same, although here indeed the tones of Cervantes are purposely less forceful. It is in the creation of atmosphere where Fielding greatly succeeds in recapturing the best of *Don Quixote*. A passage from the novel is indicative of this atmosphere. In Book IX, chapter II, Tom comes upon the suffering Mrs. Waters. With Quixotic impulse he dashes up to her rescue: "Jones asked no questions at this interval, but fell instantly upon the villain, and made such good use of his trusty oaken stick that he laid him sprawling on the ground before he could defend himself.... The poor wretch [Mrs. Waters] then fell upon her knees to Jones, and gave him a thousand thanks for her deliverance...."[28]

In the three works a development in Cervantes' influence on the English novelist grows increasingly evident. Fielding has progressed from a rough outline placed in an English setting to a withdrawal from open imitation of Cervantes. Then, while

---

[28] Henry Fielding, *The History of Tom Jones, A Foundling* (New York, [n. d.]), p. 419.

relying rather on his own genius, he has become even more deeply imbued with a Cervantean spirit. [29]

Smollett and Sterne are two other novelists who show an admiration for Cervantes to the extent that they openly incorporate characteristics of his personages in their works. Smollett is quite taken with the Spanish novelist — it is he, too, who makes a translation in this period. [30] For the purposes of this book it is not necessary to study these two writers in any detail. They do show, however, how *Don Quixote* and its author exert a very forceful sway over English letters of the day.

It was said earlier in this chapter that *Don Quixote*'s fate in seventeenth-century England was much less happy than it was in France. However, in the second hundred years of the novel's existence, the important investigations occur principally in England — not in Spain or France. At the same time, the influence of Cervantes' manner takes over certain writers to an extent that is hardly possible in the latter countries. Obviously, therefore, England has a great claim on the Spanish novel and its later propulsion to a higher level of esteem.

---

[29] For a more detailed analysis of Cervantes and Fielding, two articles are of value: A. A. Parker, "Fielding and the Structure of *Don Quixote*," *Bulletin of Hispanic Studies*, XXXIII, 1 (1956), 1-16; Homer Goldberg, "The Interpolated Stories in *Joseph Andrews* or 'The History of the World in General' Satirically Revised," *Modern Philology*, LXIII, 4 (1966), 295-310.

[30] "Smollett's hack school was either totally or partially responsible for his translation of *Don Quixote*." (Carmine Rocco Linsalata, *Smollett's Hoax: Don Quixote in English* (Stanford, 1956), pp. 22-23.)

III

THE EARLIEST MANUSCRIPT AND THE FINAL FORM OF BOWLE'S EDITION

In the previous chapter we noted the course of Cervantean criticism throughout the seventeenth and the eighteenth centuries. Now in this third chapter we return to a more detailed analysis of Bowle's edition to see how the editor and his work fit into the development of this criticism.

To know more precisely what is to be found in the edition, I shall describe its physical appearance.[1] The edition appeared in 1781 in two printings. The first printing was done entirely in Salisbury and consisted of three volumes divided into four *tomos*. The title page of Volume I reads HISTORIA/ DEL FAMOSO CAVALLERO,/ DON QUIXOTE DE LA MANCHA./ Por/ Miguel De Cervantes Saavedra./ Primera Parte. Primero Tomo./ (Design of a bull's head with garlands hanging from its horns.)/ En Salisbury:/ En la Imprenta de Edvardo Easton. M.DCC.LXXXI. (A flowered, wreathed border surrounds the page.) Opposite the title page is a map of Spain. Following the title page is the dedication in English by Bowle to the Earl of Huntington dated St. George's Day, 1781. There follow the Dedication by Cervantes to the Duque de Béjar, Cervantes' Prologue to Part I, poems, the text of Part I of *Don Quixote* (pp. 1-544), and the table of contents.

---

[1] These descriptions are based on copies in the Hispanic Society of America in New York City.

Volume II has the same title page as Volume I except it reads erroneously *Primera Parte. Segundo Tomo*. It contains Cervantes' Dedication to the Conde de Lemos, his Prologue to Part II, the text of Part II (pp.1-572), and the table of contents.

Volume III is composed entirely of Bowle's own investigations. There is an initial title page as in the other two volumes except it reads erroneously *Segunda Parte. Tercero Tomo*. The second title page says ANOTACIONES/ A LA/ HISTORIA/ DE/ DON QUIXOTE DE LA MANCHA./ Por el Reverendo/ D. Juan Bowle, A.M.S.S.A.L./ Libera per vacuum posui vestigia princeps,/ Non aliena, meo pressi pede.———Horat./ Por caminos desusados, por atajos, y sendas encubiertas.———D. Quixote, P.2./ En Salisbury:/ En la Imprenta de Edvardo Easton. M.DCC.LXXXI. After this title page is the *Prólogo Del Editor*, signed Juan Bowle, Abril 23. Por la Fiesta de San Jorge. Año de 1781 (pp. i-xiv). On pages xv-xxi are the *Autores citados en las Anotaciones*, and at the bottom of page xxi and on page xxii are the *Omisiones En Las Anotaciones*. Next are the *Anotaciones A Don Quixote* (pp. 1-157) and the *Anotaciones A Don Quixote, Segunda Parte* (new pagination: 1-167), signed: Juan Bowle, Idemestone, en su Estudio, Y Octubre 26, M.DCC.LXXX. There follow a blank page, several pages of *Subscribers*, a *Prologo A Los Indices* (pp. i-iii, signed Juan Bowle, Abril 23. Fiesta de San Jorge, 1781.), a page of *Abreviaturas en las Anotaciones é Indices* and *Palabras Ilustradas En Las Anotaciones que no se hallan en los Indices*, and the title page to the fourth *tomo*, just like that in Volume I but reading erroneously *Segunda Parte. Quarto Tomo*. There is another title page: INDICES/ DE NOMBRES PROPRIOS,/ DE PALABRAS MAS NOTABLES,/ Y VARIAS LECCIONES,/ EN ENTRAMBAS PARTES DE LA/ HISTORIA/ DE/ DON QUIXOTE DE LA MANCHA./ Por El Reverendo/ D. Juan Bowle, A.M.S.S.A.L./ Los que hacen Repertorios á los Libros son ganapanes, que/ trabajan para los demas. Fajardo. Rep. Lit. 63./ En Salisbury:/ En la Imprenta de Edvardo Easton, á costa del Editor./ M.DCC.LXXXI. The rest of the volume is composed of various indexes: *Indice De Nombres Proprios En Don Quixote. Primera Parte*. (unnumbered); *Indice De Nombres Proprios En Don Quixote. Segunda parte*. (unnumbered); *Indice De Los*

Nombres Propios En Entrambas Partes de Don Quixote. (unnumbered); *Indice De Las Palabras Principales En Don Quixote. Segunda Parte.* (unnumbered); *Varias Lecciones En Esas Ediciones De Don Quixote. Primera Parte; Varias Lecciones En Don Quixote. Segunda Parte.* (both unnumbered); and a page of Errata.

The volumes are bound in green leather with lettering in gold. The print is clear although errors exist. The division of the *tomos* is designated incorrectly in Volumes II and III.

The next printing came out in a very short time and is of interest because the first *tomo* was printed in London. This printing is also in three volumes but is divided into six *tomos*. Evidently it is the more available edition as it is the one most often listed in library catalogs.[2] By dividing the edition into six *tomos* instead of four, the errors in the first printing were removed. The texts and the pagination basically are the same, the only outstanding differences being in the number of *tomos* and in the physical appearance of the edition. This second printing is in brown leather with gold lettering. Although the pages are not so neatly cut as in the first, in general the second printing is more attractive.

Volume I of the second printing has an initial page with no ornamentation reading HISTORIA/ DEL FAMOSO CAVALLERO/ DON QUIXOTE DE LA MANCHA:/ Por/ Miguel De Cervantes Saavedra./ Con/ Anotaciones, Indices, Y Varias Lecciones:/ Por El Reverendo/ D. Juan Bowle, A.M.S.S.A.L./ En Seis Tomos. The title page differs slightly from that of the first printing: HISTORIA/ DEL FAMOSO CAVALLERO,/ DON QUIXOTE DE LA MANCHA./ Por/ Miguel De Cervantes Saavedra./ Primera Parte. Primero Tomo./ (Design which appears on Cuesta's editions.)/ En Londres: Se hallarán en las Librerias de B. White,

---

[2] Copies of Bowle's edition are found in twelve libraries in the United States. Of these, most, like the New York Public Library, have only the second printing. The Hispanic Society of America, on the other hand, has both. The libraries are Western Reserve University (Cleveland), Boston Public Library, Harvard University, University of Pennsylvania (Philadelphia), Library Company (Philadelphia), Yale University, Hispanic Society of America, University of Michigan (Ann Arbor), New York Public Library, Princeton University, University of California (Berkeley), and the Boston Athenaeum.

P./ Elmsley, T. y T. Payne, y J. Robson. M.DCC.LXXXI. There is a very elaborate border consisting of drawings of trees and armor. Although this title page has *Londres* on it, the other title pages have *Salisbury*. After this particular title page is a page with a small print of English countryside: in the lower left-hand corner is a shield bearing the initials E.B.J. and under the print is written *Edward Basil Jupp. F.S.A.* [Fellow of the Society of Antiquaries]. On the next page is the Dedication to the Earl of Huntington but much more elaborately executed. The dedication itself is in longhand and is much more formal in appearance than that of the first printing. Above the dedication is a print of the castle and coat of arms of the patron. The rest of the volume is like that of the first printing except that between pages 256 and 257 (between chapters XXVII and XXVIII) there is the second title page reading *Primera Parte. Segundo Tomo.*

The second volume contains Part II of *Don Quixote*. The title page is like that of the first printing but with *Segunda Parte. Tercero Tomo.* After Cervantes' Dedication to the Conde de Lemos and his Prologue comes the page containing the small print with *Edward Basil Jupp. F.S.A.* written at the bottom. Between pages 266 and 267 (between chapters XXXIII and XXXIV) is the title page with *Segunda Parte. Quarto Tomo.*

Volume III differs only slightly from Volume III of the first printing. First is a page with the print and the name *Edward Basil Jupp. F.S.A.* The title page reads as its earlier corresponding one. Where before there was a blank page after the *Anotaciones* to Parts I and II, now there is the title page: INDICES/ DE NOMBRES PROPRIOS,/ DE PALABRAS MAS NOTABLES,/ Y VARIAS LECCIONES,/ EN ENTRAMBAS PARTES DE LA/ HISTORIA/ DE/ DON QUIXOTE DE LA MANCHA./ Por El Reverendo/ D. Juan Bowle, A.M.S.S.A.L./ Los que hacen Reportorios á los Libros son ganapanes, que/ trabajan para los demas. Fajardo. Rep. Lit. 63./ En Salisbury:/ En la Imprenta de Edvardo Easton, á costa del Editor. M.DCC.LXXXI. Then follow the pages of *Subscribers,* the *Prologo A Los Indices,* the *Indices,* etc. The only difference here is that the map found at the beginning of Volume I of the first printing is in Volume III of the second printing between the fifth and sixth sheets of the *Indice De Nombres Proprios En Don Quixote. Primera Parte.*

At first glance, the indexes are very imposing. They occupy half of the third volume, sharing equal space with the *Anotaciones*. Much of the material is needlessly duplicated, however; as seen in the description above, the first three indexes overlap each other. The first concerns proper names in Part I and the second, those in Part II, while the third has those used in both parts. At the very end of the *Indices* some pages of correlations among various editions of *Don Quixote* are included. Even though the collection is relatively small and by modern standards would be considered very incomplete, it is important in that it unites in a group some of the textual differences found in several editions of *Don Quixote*. It is unfortunate, however, that the study comes after the *Indices* since it tends to be overlooked because of its location.

The indexes alone are not worthy of lengthy comment or study, and for this reason have not been discussed any more here. Yet one does not wish to minimize their importance in connection with the rest of the work. When they are considered together with the *Anotaciones* as part of a new kind of edition of *Don Quixote*, they help place Bowle and his work in the forefront of eighteenth-century Cervantean investigations. If they are somewhat superficial, their newness in form and content is nevertheless enough to merit our admiration.

The discussion so far has concerned the edition only as it appeared in 1781. For his preliminary work Bowle used an edition of *Don Quixote* by Pedro Alonso y Padilla which came out in 1750. The Hispanic Society of America possesses the particular copy of the Padilla edition in which Bowle wrote his notes. At the death of the founder of the Society, Archer M. Huntington, an inventory was made of the latter's private library. In it was found the manuscript of what later became Bowle's 1781 edition. The text itself is not the most legible; in fact, it is very smeared in many instances. Errors in print and in text abound. Why Bowle should have chosen such a poor and late edition cannot be definitely ascertained. It is known, however, that Bowle had had a profound knowledge of *Don Quixote* for some time and in the

1760's he had definitely decided to make his edition. When he started his actual labor on the edition, he was more concerned with his investigations of the romances of chivalry and other source books which form the core of all his endeavors. The problem in the 1760's, therefore, was not so much to have an early, reliable edition of *Don Quixote* at hand as to have any text at all which could be obtained easily. This turned out to be that of Alonso y Padilla. [3]

Bowle took this edition, underlined words and passages, and made marginal notes. More lengthy notes and quotations were put on separate sheets of paper. These later were bound within the 1750 edition. The inserted leaves are of a stronger, coarser quality than the original pages of the text. It was difficult to decide whether blank sheets had been inserted and then written on, or whether they had been written on first and then inserted. It was decided that the latter case was true — even though the pages and the writing on them fit between the pages of the text so neatly. The entire edition has been rebound in two enormous volumes of brown leather which read *Don Quixote Con Notas Ms.Tas*. In rebinding the two volumes, the inserts were fitted together in the proper order. There are other things, however, which indicate a little more clearly that the pages were inserted after being written. For example, the title page of Volume II has some words in ink missing at the top. These were written before the edition was rebound and were cut off in this process. Also, where the ink strokes of Bowle's pen ran off the paper, there is no smudge on the edge, thus indicating that these smudges were cut off in the rebinding.

By examining the manuscript copy carefully and then comparing it to the final edition of 1781, we can see the process by which the work was made complete. As the discussion goes on, it will be shown that this manuscript is a very early working tool. This

---

[3] It should be pointed out that there are in existence two handwritten books belonging to Bowle containing many of the proverbs and quotations he collected over the years and put in his edition of *Don Quixote*. The first, dated 1773 and now in the British Museum Library, is entitled *Liber Memorandorum Et Referentiarum*. The second, dated 1786, is in the possession of Professor John Bowle, a descendant of the Rev. John Bowle. This interesting book is entitled *Memorandorum Et Referentiarum Liber Alter*.

should be kept in mind as the comparison is made, for there are many divergences between the notes of the manuscript and those of the 1781 edition.

A very painless way to see the growth of the edition is to examine the list of authors whom Bowle utilized as his sources. On the inserted pages for these authors in the manuscript, there is no alphabetical order within the letters themselves. The books of *Amadís* are given first, followed by Alemán, Alfonso Lux, Acosta, and others. This indicates that the editor jotted them down as he happened to think of each. The works listed under "B" are even more confused. For example, Boscán has a prominent notice: "Boscan. Las obras de y algunas de Garcilaso de la Vega. 1547." Yet Boscán has no entry in the list of authors in the 1781 edition, although there is one for Garcilaso (the 1622 edition of his poems).

Whereas the works of Cervantes are listed under his name in the 1750 manuscript, they are given by the titles in the 1781 edition. The listing in the manuscript is not nearly so complete for Cervantes, and the want of organization in compiling his works is more apparent also.

At times the titles of books (especially of the romances of chivalry) are much longer in the manuscript, but in the final edition they are greatly shortened. Further polishing of the edition is seen in the moving of *L'Histoire Palladienne* from "H" to "P," in the addition of Hyginus to the final edition, and in the addition of a whole new series of "C's" after *La Pícara Justina*. This new list includes two very significant works: *La Celestina* and the *Cancionero de Anvers* (or *Cancionero de Romances*, as Bowle more often calls it).

Showing the passage of time during which all this material was accumulated, Sarmiento's name is not mentioned in the 1750 work, but it stands out prominently in the 1781 edition. Fray Martín Sarmiento had made a great impression on Bowle because of his investigations to determine Cervantes' birthplace. His findings were published in 1777 as *Noticia de la verdadera Patria (Alcalá) de "El" Miguel de Cerbantes* (Madrid: 18 de Junio, 1777).

The picture which results from studying the *Autores Citados* as given in the manuscript copy is one of chaos — there seems to be a complete lack of direction in the editor's method of compiling source materials. The editor also fails to number the pages and this tends to heighten the effect of confusion. This disorder is not just a characteristic of the list of authors, for it continues in the arrangement of all notes in the manuscript. More than anything, it is due to the insertion of the sheets of notes after the notes were made. In addition, since in the beginning pages there is no number to indicate the page of the text to which the note refers, the want of clarity is heightened even more. The only saving grace is that in nearly all cases the phrases or sentences commented on are underlined in the text, and this helps in locating the passage. Still, one must go leafing through sometimes twenty pages to place a reference with the textual lines. Most of this trouble has been caused by inserting the sheets as they are found now. Yet, such criticism is somewhat unfair because this is the manuscript copy in its very earliest stages and it was meant for Bowle's reference and not the ordinary reader's.

Besides the problems resulting from the notes, the format of the text of Padilla's edition is different from that of the 1781 work, and this causes some difficulty when relating the manuscript notes to the text of both Padilla's and Bowle's final editions. The 1750 edition has a title page after which comes the homage supposedly by Cide Hamete. The dedication to the Duque de Béjar is missing as are all the laudatory poems. Before Cervantes' prologue and in the midst of Cide Hamete's homage, some of the sheets of notes are inserted in a rather disorderly fashion. Since the sheets have comments on the poems not found in the 1750 edition, much confusion results in trying to ascertain the development of the comments.

The material which Bowle presents as sources and references for the prologue is much more extensive in the 1781 edition. Many changes and omissions occur between the manuscript and the final work. The note for "Al Duque de Béjar" from the dedication is not in the manuscript. The reason undoubtedly is that this dedication is not in the 1750 edition.

In addition to the disorder exhibited in the manuscript notes, the different shades of ink in which the notes are written pose some problems. The ink evidently was all black at one time but has faded according to the size of the point of the pen and the pressure with which the letters were written. Some of the notes are in an ink so faded as to appear nearly brown, while others are in a blunt, deep black. On page 14b (pages unless marked "II" will mean Part I: page 14, "b" being the verso side of the first inserted sheet following page 14) there is a series of notes, all in different shades of black ink. The handwriting is smaller and more cramped in some of the references, probably showing more concentration as later notes were added to an increasingly filled page. Many of the quotations from ballads are in the very faded ink. I would assume that since the quotations from nearly all the *romances* seem to have been written earlier, simply because of a neater arrangement on the page, the lighter ink indicates earlier notation. There is hardly a single insert which does not have different inks on it with the blacker ink strokes at times running boldly over the lighter. This too would point to a reworking of the manuscript copy over a period of years.

Another curious circumstance is the lines drawn through certain references. On page 16b there is a note for "hato." It is a definition from Covarrubias reading "vale cantidad de cabeças de ganado, cómo *hato* de ovejas, de cabras." This definition has been omitted from the 1781 edition, and by the reference in the manuscript a circle is drawn with a soft brown pencil. Other notes on page 16b have straight lines drawn through them, and these particular notes are used in the 1781 edition. The notes on page 18b are in different shades of ink and show reworkings in several instances. All of them have lines through them in black or brown pencil. However, only two out of the seven on the page are used in the final work. On page 22b there are two quotations — unmarked and not in the 1781 edition. Neither is very appropriate and gives no real explanation of the text. For this reason Bowle must have later deemed it wiser to omit them.

The quotations on page 32: 40-7 (this designation means *Anotaciones* for Part I, page 32, page 40 of the 1781 text of *Don Quixote,* and line 7 of that page) for "Turpin" are on page 30b of the 1750 edition. The first of the poems (from *Silva de Romances*) is in a more faded ink than the others. Those from Pulci are much darker and obviously later. All of these have a line drawn through them. Also the prose lines from *Turpinus* are more closely spaced than those mentioned above and would indicate that Bowle was being more pressed for space when he reached this reference.

In general, those passages with straight lines through them are in the 1781 edition. The lines and circles are meant to indicate inclusion in, or deletion from, the 1781 edition. Even though this statement does not hold true rigidly in all cases (as seen in the few examples above), it covers the majority of the references.

There is another characteristic of the 1750 edition which helps indicate Bowle's particular train of thought when he was writing his notes. In several instances Bowle corrects errors in Padilla's 1750 text, and in others he fails to do so. This does not indicate so much a lack of knowledge on Bowle's part as it does a different direction of interest at the time the specific note was made. When writing any given note, he may not he concerned necessarily with textual inaccuracy. And later he may or may not correct the text. These idiosyncrasies aid in showing the long period in which the notes were produced. As an example of this passage of time, on page 14b Bowle writes "tiendas de Sanchominaya" — exactly as the 1750 text reads. The quotation he puts here appears just as it does in the 1781 edition (22: 19-27), but, in the latter, Bowle corrects the textual quotation to read "Sanchobienaya." The ink in the manuscript for this particular reference is very faded, with a later addition in blacker ink of "Pisa" at the end. The word *Pisa* is in the 1781 text. Its addition in the 1750 notes with blacker ink helps to prove that Bowle returned to the manuscript copy often for the insertion of newly found information.

Page 67 of the 1750 text has "el espantable *Valando* de algun monstruo." Bowle, in a note on the facing page (66b), has written "el espantable baladro." This is the correct reading, and it appears thus in the 1781 edition. Bowle makes no correction in the Padilla text itself, however. It is only by the note on the facing page that we know he is aware of the error. He points out this difference in the *Varias Lecciones* at the end of Volume III of the 1781 edition as well — Madrid 1605 having *balando* and Valencia 1608, *baladro*.

In the final edition of 1781 Bowle has very few of his personal remarks and sentiments. To an extent this is not quite true of the manuscript, for in the latter what observations he does have are more spontaneous than their 1781 counterparts. A statement about Amadís' habit of crying when emotionally upset is much more energetic in the manuscript, for example: (page 4a) "Esta observacion acerca el caracter de Amadis es muy justa: en su historia esta casi siempre llorando: Estas partes abasten para confirmacion desto ...." Compare these lines to the 1781 statement: (8: 3-13) "Basten estos pasos de su historia para confirmacion de lo que se dice aquí ...."

His comments on Avellaneda's Part II also change slightly as time passes. The manuscript sounds more forthright and more impulsive: "El character deste libro [Avellaneda's] es una excepcion a su regla, y *es tan malo que no tenga en si cosa alguna buena.*" (II, page 330a). The 1781 notes have: (139: 61-19, 20; Part II) "Lo que escrivió *Cervantes* de este maldito libro se dixo con toda verdad y sin colera." In the same chapter (Part II, LIX) Cervantes makes another remark about Avellaneda's work. Bowle writes in the manuscript: (II, 332b) "Los torpissimos Adulterios, y Homicidios hazen los sujetos de dos feissimos cuentos sin ningun proposito, ni moral, que se hallan en este maldito libro." The final edition has: (141: 465-1; Part II) "Los mas torpes Adulterios, y Homicidios, hacen los sugetos de dos Cuentos, sin ningun proposito, ni moral, en este libro, tan justamente menoscabado de todos hombres de buen gusto."

All along we have seen how there has been a gradual development of Bowle's work from his manuscript notes in Padilla's 1750 edition of *Don Quixote* to his own final edition in 1781. The conclusion is that the manuscript in the Hispanic Society is a working copy, containing the earliest annotations which were later reworked. Two further observations concerning the notes give more force to this conclusion. Of the notes which are in the 1781 edition and not found in the manuscript copy, many are from Covarrubias. Also, many of the notes merely refer to works cited elsewhere in the *Anotaciones*. The insertion of these two types of notes in the final edition strengthens the idea that the 1750 edition was a working tool during the collection of material over a period of years. The 1750 text, therefore, served as a vehicle for the first information and also for the most basic.

This ends the more detailed study of the physical appearance of the 1781 edition and its origins. Yet a very essential question concerning the texts Bowle used for Parts I and II of Don Quixote in his edition has still not been discussed. For some unfortunate reason, Bowle does not state in his prologue exactly which texts he used. Except for one aside in the notes he says nothing. Within the Anotaciones on 153: 518-22 he writes: "*por muchos y diversos exemplos*) — y las seis lineas siguientes solamente se hallan en la *Impresion de 1608, que ha sido principalmente seguida en esta* [italics mine]." Since this is the only allusion he makes to his choice of text, we must accept the statement as it stands. At least it comes from the editor himself. Some bibliographers, such as Rius and Río y Rico, believe that Bowle used the 1608 edition of Part I and the 1615 edition of Part II as the base texts. [4]

Some comparisons made among early editions substantiate these statements. In the *Varias Lecciones* at the end of Volume III Bowle compares certain variants among selected editions: Part I — Madrid, 1605; Valencia, 1605; Madrid, 1608; Londres, 1738; Part II — Madrid, 1615; Valencia, 1616; Londres, 1738. The Madrid 1605 is the second edition of Cuesta and the 1608 edition, his third. For Part II, the Madrid 1615 is the first, also by Cuesta. Taking the 1605 and 1608 editions and following most of the variants listed for Part I and employing some at random, it was discovered that Bowle's text agrees in every case with the 1608 edition and not with the Madrid 1605. Of great importance among these variants is the one about Sancho and his donkey. Where the Madrid 1605 edition has "siguióle Sancho *con su acostumbrado jumento*," the 1608 edition has the obviously needed correction: "siguióle Sancho *á pie, y cargado.*" Bowle notes this glaring error and is certainly one of the first to do so.

It is a little startling, nevertheless, that the variants all point to the 1608 edition because Bowle in his *Letter to the Reverend Dr. Percy* in 1777 had indicated that he would follow the Madrid

---

[4] Gabriel Martín del Río y Rico, *Catálogo bibliográfico de la sección de Cervantes de la Biblioteca Nacional* (Madrid, 1930), p. 41.

1605 edition: "As it is my ultimate wish to have the text pure and genuine, I would spare no pains to effect this. For which purpose, the first [but actually Cuesta's second], printed in Madrid 1605, in quarto, by Juan de la Cuesta, seems to merit the preference: this I have very carefully collated ...." [5]

The solution is that between 1777 and 1781 Bowle studied more editions, even the Valencia 1605 and the Madrid 1608 which in 1777 had "never yet come to my inspection ..." [6] and finally based his text for Part I on the 1608 edition with reference to the others mentioned.

For Part II, Bowle's text follows the first edition of 1615 (Cuesta's), except in two places where his text agrees with the 1616 Valencia edition. In chapter XXII Bowle has "le dexaron calar" for "le dexó calar" of the 1615 edition. In the same chapter he agrees with the 1616 "con grande atencion escuchavan" as opposed to the 1615 "con cuchavan." One is at a loss to explain these differences. Since Bowle's renderings are clearer and since the two editions generally are very similar, it may be that he chose the 1616 version as more logical. Yet this is pure conjecture. At any rate, the 1608 Madrid edition of Cuesta is the basis for Part I, and the 1615 Madrid edition of Cuesta is the basis for Part II. This assertion corroborates those of Rius and Río y Rico — as well as Bowle's own regarding Part I. [7]

---

[5] John Bowle, *A Letter to the Reverend Dr. Percy, Concerning a New and Classical Edition of Historia Del Valeroso Cavallero Don Quixote De La Mancha* (London, 1777), p. 33.

[6] *Ibid.*, p. 34.

[7] Dr. Serís points out that Bowle was the first to realize that there was another 1605 Cuesta edition besides the one with the *Privilegio* for Portugal of February 9, 1605. This latter edition was accepted as the first up through the eighteenth century. Bowle does not really alter this belief; but, in an easily overlooked statement in his prologue, he mentions the real first edition while describing the edition with the *Privilegio* for Portugal: "... será bien nombrar las Ediciones originales: y primeramente [speaking of the second Cuesta edition, thinking it the first]:
EL INGENIOSO HIDALGO DON QUIXOTE DE LA MANCHA. *Compuesto por Miguel de Cervantes Saavedra.* Año 1605. En MADRID, Por Juan de la Cuesta, 4to. *Consta que uvo otra del mismo año, lugar, y forma* [italics mine]." (Volume III, *Prólogo* to the *Anotaciones a Don Quixote*, p. ix).
Bowle for the first time notes what later is proved to be the true first edition. Bowle knew very little about the edition, though, and had never

seen it. At least he does more than his immediate successors who only follow what he says. It is not until 1826 that Vicente Salvá resolves the problem. He sees that the *corrector* of the edition with the *Privilegio* only for Castilla (the real first edition) had dated his *Testimonio de las erratas* December 1, 1604. The edition which Bowle refers to above with "primeramente" and which he uses in the *Varias Lecciones* has the *Privilegio* for Castilla, Aragón, and Portugal dated February 9, 1605, thus making it impossible for it to be first. These two editions are the first and second of Juan de la Cuesta. (Homero Serís, "La colección Cervantina de la Sociedad Hispánica de América," *University of Illinois. Studies in Language and Literature,* VI (Urbana, 1920), pp. 17-18.)

IV

THE EDITOR'S CONCEPTION OF *DON QUIXOTE*

We have placed Bowle's edition of *Don Quixote* chronologically within its period and in a very general fashion have seen how the edition is constructed. We can now look in more detail at Bowle's ideas and attitudes concerning the work he edited. From the first, his intention was to produce an edition which would clarify confusions and vague references in *Don Quixote*. In addition, he would seek to present all the source materials which Cervantes could have used in writing the novel.

For the first time, as a result of Bowle's ideas, a classical edition is made of *Don Quixote*. It is natural to expect an edition like Bowle's at some time in the eighteenth century, and it does not seem at all strange that such a work should come from England. We are amazed only that this work appears so late in the century. It is even more astonishing that nothing similar had been proposed before this time. Except for Mayáns' life of Cervantes and some minor comments in Jarvis' translation, nothing of real importance had appeared before the 1780's. Then in this particular decade there are two works: Bowle's and Vicente de los Ríos' (in 1780). Concerning preliminary investigations and extension of work, Bowle's work is much more ambitious and more firmly based. Bowle's is an edition of Cervantes' novel containing great amounts of factual material. Ríos' is not an edition in itself of *Don Quixote* but a subjective essay concerning various themes running through the novel. Ríos has no edition of the novel — although his commentary does appear in the Academy's edition of 1780.

It is rather surprising that two men should write as they do at practically the same time, especially when both attempt at last to go beneath the surface of the novel and draw out facts which had not been emphasized previously. Both have been somewhat forgotten except in isolated pockets of Cerventean investigations, although Ríos has suffered less from oblivion than Bowle.

These two scholars approach the subject from entirely different angles. Bowle's is a "classical" edition; Ríos' is not. To understand better what Bowle has done, we can use Ríos' *Análisis del Quixote* as a good contrast. When mentioning Ríos earlier in chapter II, note was made of his emphasis on the comparison between Homer and Cervantes. Like Mayáns and later Pellicer, he believes that the relationship between Homer and Cervantes is very close. While showing this relationship, Ríos states his opinions quite definitely about Cervantes and *Don Quixote*. His thoughts are personal, and, even though they often sound bombastic or incredible, they are, nevertheless, his own thoughts in his own words. This injection of the writer himself into his work is the opposite of what Bowle does. Bowle's own personal statements are few. For example, Bowle would never make such a forthright statement about Cervantes' purposes in writing *Don Quixote* as Ríos does on page c of his *Análisis del Quixote:* "Lo cierto es que el principal fin de Cervantes no fué divertir y entretener á sus lectores, como vulgarmente se cree. Valióse de este medio como de un lenitivo para templar la delicada satira que hizo de las costumbres de su tiempo...." *

Besides the differences in methods, the entire framework of the two commentaries is different. Bowle's notes are in a separate volume with references by page and line to the text of the novel. The notes are citations of similar, or of the same, words and actions in other works. Like Bowle's, Ríos' comments are in a separate volume from those containing the text of *Don Quixote*. But here the similarity ends, for Ríos approaches the novel by *artículo* or subject. *Artículo IV*, for example, is entitled

---

* Rather than have a long series of footnotes, the title, author, and page are given in the text. For more specific information, such as the edition used, the reader should see the bibliography at the end of the book.

"Caracteres de los personages de esta fábula." It is a general observation on the figures in the novel. This is not too close to Bowle's approach of chapter by chapter, line by line.

Near the end of his work Ríos gives a concise summary of his ideas. It is in his own words and is rather lengthy. In these two simple characteristics, his work differs from Bowle's. The latter does not present his material in such a way that he can summarize it, even if he were so disposed. The following long quotation is included because it states what Ríos' beliefs are. It helps to make Bowle's procedures stand out even more notably in their singularity:

> En él [Discurso] hemos descubierto, que el objeto de la Fábula de Cervantes fue nuevo y original, y más a propósito aun que el de las heroycas para enseñar deleytando: que de este objeto deduxo la accion, que es la locura de Don Quixote, accion sola, completa, de proporcionada duracion, verosímil y variada con episodios, enlazados naturalmente con ella: que los caractéres de las personas son constantes y propios de sus calidades, y de las circunstancias en que se hallan, sobresaliendo entre todos el de Don Quixote como Héroe de la fábula: que su narracion es dramática, dulce y hermosa, precedida de una proposicion sencilla y natural, correspondiente á la accion: que su estilo es puro, enérgico y conveniente á la materia: y finalmente que con la hermosura y gracia que reyna en toda la fábula, envuelve los documentos de una moral discreta y juiciosa, alabando las virtudes, y reprehendiendo los vicios; pero especialmente los que mas conexîon tenian con su asunto, que son los de la caballería andante. (pp. cxxxvi-cxxxvii).

Ríos says essentially that Cervantes wrote well. In Cervantes all the proprieties so esteemed by the correct eighteenth-century individual are to be found, for the novelist shows good judgment, good taste, and proportion. Bowle says these same things about Cervantes in his *Anotaciones*, but they are never nicely set down for us as they are here in Ríos. Bowle, in general, is too restrained to make direct comments. He seeks by more reserved means to show what *Don Quixote* is. He succeeds in his method just as Ríos succeeds in his. In essence, they both have the same purpose in mind, that of exalting their subject.

It has been remarked several times that Bowle rarely states his opinions or ideas anywhere and this reticence is all too true of the *Anotaciones* themselves. Their format nearly destroys all possibility of personal comment, for Bowle allows the collecting and presenting of quotations from other sources to exclude his own presence in his work. He much prefers a kind of editing which in itself shuts out its composer. Thus, even if Bowle's ordinary manner were one wherein he would be expected to appear boldly on the page, his approach to his edition does not allow too intimate an involvement with his subject — at least too close an involvement on the pages before us.

Again, as is the case of almost every point of investigation regarding Bowle, we must look in more detail into what he says. We cannot accept what is on the surface alone, for there is little to indicate a real person behind the elaborate façade of the notes. At first glance, one is awed at the accumulation of so many references. Our first impression is to admire the erudition and long labor of the individual who produced this somewhat ornate structure. It is only later that we begin to wonder what the editor was like and to wonder what his own ideas were. And this is when we begin to look more carefully at what is in the notes. We notice little comments, short sentences at most, where Bowle allows himself to enter his work freely. In the choice of his references we see certain trends in his thoughts. But it is not until we have looked at all the work and gone back over pages at random that we can see the directions the editor's mind is taking.

To make some of Bowle's attitudes more evident, references have been selected and arbitrarily placed under various headings. These latter will help to determine what are, or are not, his opinions. Examining his quotations from Covarrubias, for example, from the romances of chivalry, or from historical texts, we can determine where he would place *Don Quixote* in literature and, even more important, how he would fit *Don Quixote* into an historical framework. Finally, by collecting his own opinions — few as they are — and looking at them in their entirety, we shall begin to see how he lets his emotions concerning the novel emerge.

Of all the references found in the *Anotaciones,* the most noticeable are those giving definitions of words or expressions. Their ubiquitous presence becomes a little tiring after a time. Generally they come from Covarrubias, but other sources are employed too. It strikes one as odd that Bowle should give definitions of Spanish words. Since the edition is written in Spanish, the only people who might read it would necessarily have to have a sufficient knowledge of that language. Otherwise they could hardly understand what they were reading. Here appears one of the peculiarities of the edition. Bowle assumes that even Spaniards need clarification of certain now nebulous passages. This is most probably true. Yet he includes so very many comments on individual words that one senses he is writing more for the English-speaking individual — although writing in Spanish. This fault of the work — if it is a fault really — was noted immediately by early critics, particularly Baretti.

As the notation of words and short phrases is so prominent in the edition, it merits more discussion. The notes from Covarrubias, Aldrete, and Nebrija are actually the key to understanding the editor's approach to *Don Quixote*. In various places Bowle makes statements expounding his reasons for writing a commentary on the novel. The earliest and most concise of these statements is in his *Letter to Dr. Percy*. At the very end he writes: "I have only to add, that Cervantes was himself sensible that his History would need a Comment, and has told us as much by the mouth of his hero, 'que tendra necessidad de comento para entenderla....'" (page 49).

As his work progresses, however, his reasons become more specific and clear. By the time he writes the prologue to his *Anotaciones,* he can say with more justification:

> Parecera sin duda á muchos en el Orbe Literario una Empresa muy estraña el intento de un Ingles, no solamente en idear, quanto mas en acabar, y sacar á luz una Edicion Clasica de un Escritor *Español,* y de una Historia tan celebre, como la de *Don Quixote De La Mancha* ... Pero deben de advertir los tales, que el adquirir conocimiento bastante para empezar á leer con facilidad el Castellano *(y todo es comenzar)* está en poder de cada uno que sabe bien el Latín, y desea alcanzarlo. Se puede afirmar

esto con toda verdad: sin embargo, como *nadie nace enseñado,* para aprender con extension ésta, ó alguna otra lengua, se pide mucho tiempo, y mayor atencion. Darán para este fin mucha ayuda é informacion los dos Oraculos de la Castellana Don Bernardo *Aldrete,* y Don Sebastian de *Cobarruvias* Orozco. Y el *Tesoro* del postrero ha sido un verdadero tesoro para la *Glosa,* que va ingerida entre las Anotaciones, y ... da el distinto sentido de las Voces, que se usavan por el Autor.... Hallanse en el mismo Tesoro Costumbres varias; bien declaradas, que, aunque bien conocidas á los Nacionales, á Estrangeros parecerán nuevas y peregrinas, y por esta razon deben de apuntarse; porque segun el observacion del Padre Fr. Mro. Sarmiento, Mucho de lo que está vulgarizado en España suele ser ignoto en otras Naciones. Por eso, se espera que se escusarán estas noticias que trahen consigo instruccion. Es un error grande pensar, que porque una circunstancia está bien conocida á muchos, que debe de ser á todos. *En cada tierra su uso.* (pp. i-ii).

His purpose obviously is to instruct — this is clearly stated above. All of what he says points to the eighteenth-century delight in providing nice little details for the interested observer. This whole concept, so basic to the edition, is nowhere so well stated as on page six of the *Anotaciones* for Part I. On this page we see the guiding principle in his approach and the goals for which he is striving all neatly expounded: "*Varios* enredos y Dificultades se ofrecen al Lector en el Texto: allanar á estos, y quitar á aquellas, forman el intento del Autor de las Anotaciones, que van añadidas á esta gran obra: Oxala que contribuyen [sic] al gustoso entretenimiento del curioso Lector, ilustrando los pasos deste AUTOR CELEBERRIMO...."

With the references from Covarrubias and others, we are thus at the very heart of Bowle's concept of a classical edition. He finds references and entire passages in *Don Quixote* which, in his opinion, are no longer readily understood by the contemporary reader. To be comprehended, the work must have lengthy notes explaining what these passages mean. This is exactly what had been and was being done with the authors of Antiquity. The idea is that the work, because of the difficulty of its content and its age, has reached a point where it must be explained. The significant thing about Bowle is that this is the first time such an idea has occurred to anyone concerning *Don Quixote.*

The quotations below, chosen from hundreds just like them in the *Anotaciones,* illustrate this desire to explain and clarify — the most obvious characteristic of the edition. The quotations are definitions, and the first one is of interest because Bowle quotes both Nebrija and Covarrubias: (27: 69-10; Part II) "*almagre*) es una tierra colorada. *Cov.* Barro para teñir. *Nebrissensis.*" and (137: 469-14) "(*barberia*) la tienda del barbero: el arte mesma. *Nebrissensis.*"

The next quotations are of a more historical character and show the "costumbres" which Bowle notes in his prologue:

> (56: 153-6; Part II) *una danza de espadas*).... Aquellos santos padres prohibieron semejantes bailes, antigua costumbre de nuestra España, continuada desde su gentilidad, conservada en *las danzas de Espadas. Aldrete. Orig*....
>
> (65: 139-17) *nunca la lanza embotó la pluma, ni la, &c.*) Proverbio. La Pluma no *embota* la lanza. Dos principios ay de nobleza, las letras, y las armas... y el que fuere sabio y valiente tendrá lo todo. Exemplos ay assi antiguos, como modernos, de grandes principes, que igualmente usavan de la pluma, y de la lanza. *Cov.*

Bowle also makes use of a work which is of a more popular nature. This is the collection of *Refranes* compiled by Hernán Núñez. There are many proverbs in *Don Quixote,* and Bowle tries to ascertain the origins of these proverbs and, where possible, to give some authority for them. Bowle's investigation of works of various degrees of importance is noteworthy. It shows that he goes to all sources, popular as well as learned in trying to clarify and give a basis for everything which will help to place *Don Quixote* within an already existing literary tradition. Typical of this kind of reference is this familiar one: (90: 262-10; Part II) "*y que no es oro todo lo que reluce*) No es todo oro, &c. *Nuñez.* 80."

Bowle's use of the books of chivalry, the *romances,* the Italian epic poems, and books on history is indicative of his attitudes toward the Middle Ages. It is fascinating that he should mix together a fantastic kind of fiction with historical truth. All kinds of questions are brought up — the most important being what is fictional and what is true for him. It is odd that he, being so obviously a part of his century when verisimilitude is demanded above all else, should dare to combine two such opposite worlds in a learned work like his edition. From what is seen in the *Anotaciones,* he has no fixed attitude as to what is real and what is not real in the so-called Middle Ages. Since he makes no forthright statements as would Ríos, we feel to an extent handicapped in setting up an organized scheme of his ideas. But when he combines at will quotations from Mariana and *Amadís de Gaula,* for example, to explain some reference in *Don Quixote,* it is assumed that he considers the matters in each with equal faith. This does not imply that he believes the chivalric works, the *romances,* or the Italian epics are historical documents — far from it. It implies that in them he can see reflections of customs and events indicative of what occurs in *Don Quixote.* In this light he has no qualms about treating all these sources equally to prove his point — that *Don Quixote* is part of a tradition both literary and cultural. Whether his sources are all reliable historically does not bother him, therefore. The romances of chivalry and the Italian epics, along with actual historical narrative, represent a period of time. This latter is somewhat nebulous, but Bowle, like his contemporaries, finds it easy to refer to it simply as the "Middle Ages," whatever that may be.

In the poem in Part I in which "Urganda la desconocida" addresses Don Quixote, Don Álvaro de Luna is mentioned with other historical individuals. Bowle chooses quotations from Mariana: (4: xiv-10) "Don *Alvaro de Luna* abaxó la cabeza para que se la cortasen á cinco del mes de julio. 1452. Varon verdaderamente grande...." In this same poetic material when Babieca speaks with Rocinante, Bowle quotes from the *Crónica del Cid:* "Salió una yegua con un potro muy feo y sarnoso: é dixo á su padrino: Este quiero yo. E su padrino, dixole con saña: Babieca, mal escogistes...." (5: xx-7). In making these comments, Bowle has relied on an historical source in one instance and a fabricated text in the other. Bowle comes back to the *Crónica* repeatedly. Later when defining what is meant by "á mi tizona" (54: 109-4), he writes ".... Del Rey Juñez ganó el Cid á la su noble *espada,* á quien dizen *Tizona."*

To identify Claridiana (5: xix-10), he goes to the *Caballero del Febo:* "Sabed que yo me llamo Claridiana, y soy hija del Emperador Theodoro de este Imperio de Trapisonda...." *Tirante el Blanco* and *Historia del Emperador Carlo Magno* are used much in the same way on pages 30: 36-19 and 41: 61-28. These references give a concise idea of how Bowle uses this kind of work although the novels appear much more prominently throughout the *Anotaciones* than these few examples would imply. Practically every known book of chivalry is cited at some time or other.

The *romances,* which are scattered about for all kinds of illustrations, hold a strategic place in the notes also. They are interesting because this is the first time they have been greatly used in a learned edition. For many of these quotations Bowle employs the *Cancionero de Anvers* (thus cited in the *Anotaciones*). The appearance of the *romances* indicates an interest in them for reasons other than their being a manifestation of popular poetry. In his own way Bowle is contributing to the re-evaluation of this Medieval material. Although his efforts are less spectacular than those of Tomás Antonio Sánchez, he is effecting much the same thing. Typical of so many of the quotations from the ballads is this one: (26: 63-23; Part II) "*Romance, que dice, mala la huvistes Franceses en esa de Roncesvalles)* Romance del Conde Guarinos Almirante de la Mar: trata como lo cativaron los Moros./ *Mala la vistes Franceses/ La caza de Ronces valles/* Don Carlos perdio la honra...."

Bowle is endowing these poems with a certain historical flavor just by including them in the *Anotaciones.* They provide him with a source for remarks in *Don Quixote.* Very indirectly, he is saying that the *romances* give historical veracity for a period too long misconceived. In using the *romances* in this way — something rarely done before him — Bowle is anticipating to a degree the effusion of reverence which these poems will receive from the Romantics. It illustrates again the building of strong foundations in the eighteenth century for many of the characteristics of early nineteenth-century literary attitudes. Although not too overtly showing his participation, Bowle is profoundly involved in this new movement.

Quotations from Italian epics are just as abundant as those from the romances of chivalry and the *romances*. Boiardo and Ariosto are the writers most referred to by Bowle. A source for *Don Quixote* is found in Boiardo for lines on Tristan and Iseult (149: 511-23): "*los amores de Don Tristan, y la Reina Iseo, como los de Ginebra, y Lanzarote*) .... Saran sempre in terra nominati/ Tristano, é Isotta fior d'ogni bellezza,/ *Gineura, é Lancilotto.*" A somewhat far-fetched comparison is made between Cervantes and Ariosto in 89: 209-18: "*y quien lo contrario entendiere, miente*) .... Il conte piu non tacque, é grido forte,/ E tu, é qualunque il dice, se ne *miente*." Pulci is cited quite often. And one of the most beautiful selections occurs in a comparison of the language of Cervantes and Pulci (14: 8-11) "*la rosada Aurora, que dexando la blanca cama del zeloso Marido*) Era il sol al balcon d'oriente/ El'Aurora si facea vermiglia,/ E da Triton suo antico un poco assente." If Ríos, Pellicer, or Clemencín had cited this passage, they would have mentioned the flowery style and how it has even corrupted Cervantes. Bowle, however, never considers this worthy of comment.

Returning to more "historical" sources, we have a selection from Cascales and one from *Las Siete Partidas*. We find these sources included with the kind of material already mentioned, with which they are considered to be of equal significance:

> (24: 25-2) *comprar seda á Murcia*) No se puede passar en silencio *el trato de la seda de Murcia,* pues en ella se exercita mas que en otra parte de España, i con mayor abundancia. *Fr. Cascales. Discursos de Murcia*....
>
> (94: 269-26; Part I) *el exercicio de la caza de monte es el mas conveniente, y necessario para los Reyes y Principes que otro alguno. La caza es una imagen de la guerra*) Los antiguos tuvieron que conviene esto mucho á los Reyes *mas que á otros omes. La caza es arte, é sabiduria de guerrear, é de vencer*.... *Partidas.* 2 Tit. v. Ley XX.

As a final illustration of the historical material, there is another selection from Ariosto. It is included here because it exemplifies so well the close mingling of history and myth which Bowle has been allowing: (145: 500-11) "*en tiempo del Rey Pepino, y Carlo*

Magno) Re Carlo figlio de Pepino. Ariosto.... Murió Pepino año de 768. Carlo Magno en 814."

This quotation from Ariosto is not out of place and it explains what is in the novel. It also serves to conclude Bowle's thoughts on the Middle Ages and on *Don Quixote*'s relation to history and fiction. The addition of the dates in the above reference is very intriguing. Unconsciously, Bowle's somewhat careless joining of an historical statement to a line from Ariosto proves his failure to distinguish between fact and myth. Because of his use of this one source we may at last define his attitude. Cervantes' novel is for Bowle much like all these selections accumulated here. It is a mélange of the real and the unreal. It is a pleasant combination of the ordinary and the fantastic. It thus contains what is contemporary, whether it is true or not. In the sense that Bowle has allowed this combination in order to place *Don Quixote* more properly within a literary framework, he has accepted all these works as valid literary productions. There is no condemnation of any of them as fantastic or lacking in artistic merits. There is simply an acceptance of them as necessary in the genesis of Cervantes' work. For this reason we cannot say that Bowle condemns them at all, morally (as was most common in the case of the chivalric books) or otherwise. He is endowing the romances of chivalry, especially, with much more prestige than they had enjoyed before him. In this he goes beyond the Romantics, who will still laugh at the novels though they will venerate the period which the novels supposedly portray. In his own manner, therefore, Bowle very quietly goes beyond contemporary scholars and, in a rather unorthodox way, evinces an extraordinarily modern spirit in his fairness and candor.

It has been noted several times thus far that Bowle rarely makes judgments of his own. In producing his classical edition he sticks rigidly to passages from other authors. It must not be inferred, however, that he never injects his own comments at all, for he does permit himself the liberty of speaking out on various occasions. After the more significant comments have been accumulated (nearly all, except some of only a word or two) and regarded as a whole, certain further conclusions can be made about the editor's attitude toward *Don Quixote*. These remarks range from those that are completely superfluous to some few that show real insight. In them we get some notion as to what Bowle's ideas about the characters themselves are. Very hesitantly, Bowle begins to see in the character of Don Quixote a transcendent figure. In Sancho he begins to see a sturdy, astute individual who is a good contrast to his too visionary master. In presenting these ideas — ever so timidly, to be sure — he shows both a keen insight and a lyrical emotionalism which rarely comes to the surface. Yet as we study the quotations below, we must be wary of seeing too much in them. Their content is veiled, and Bowle himself most likely does not fully realize the impact of what he is saying. We are only on the threshold of new interpretations at this time. With Bowle we cannot take the full plunge from the restrained vision of the eighteenth century into the more liberal interpretations of the novel and its characters on the part of the Romantic school in the next century.

By examining first the statements of a less personal character and then progressing to the more personal ones, we shall see the process whereby Bowle delves more deeply into what is in the novel and its characters. The following quotation is like many which Bowle uses to show the sources of some of Cervantes' tales. Yet it is different too in that in this particular instance he states that the Spanish author most likely did not know the source. It involves Don Quixote's speech on arms and letters (Part I, chapter XXXVIII) (122: 390-21): "Hallase en Italiano — Discurso di *Francesco Bocchi* Sopra la lite delle Armi, & delle Lettere; Et á cui si dee il primo luogo di nobilta attribuire. In *Fiorenza*. 1580.... No es de creerse que jamás vió este libro *Cervantes*." Bowle almost imperceptibly interjects his comment.

The delving into the nature of the characters in the novel is most in evidence with regard to Sancho. Yet it is only after reviewing all the editor's comments that we begin to notice an understanding of the squire. When noting some lines concerning Sancho's supposed visit to Dulcinea (Part I, chapter XXXI), Bowle writes: (111: 298-24, 6) "Esta es parte de la *fingida respuesta* .... de Sancho, que *miente* ... aquí .... Dice Quixote: *Dulcinea no sabe escrivir, ni leer.*" In the verb *miente* Bowle is being rather severe in his judgment of Sancho. Sancho is "lying" certainly, but Bowle's statement is a little harsh. Nevertheless, the bluntness of the editor persists throughout his statements. As he progresses in his study of the novel, and permits himself these comments, we find that he evinces more and more of an involvement with and an admiration for Sancho.

Finally in chapter LXXII of Part II Bowle makes a statement which shows the affection that all along has been increasing in him for Don Quixote's squire. In this chapter Don Alvaro Tarfe arrives at the inn where Don Quixote and Sancho are staying. He is a principal character in Avellaneda's Part II, having encouraged the latter's Don Quixote to go to Zaragoza. He is engaged in conversation now by Don Quixote and Sancho, who ask him if they at all resemble their counterparts in Avellaneda's work. The gentleman replies in the negative and adds that although Avellaneda's Sancho "tenía fama de muy gracioso, nunca le oí decir gracia que la tuviese." Sancho replies: "Eso creo yo muy bien ... porque el decir gracias no es para todos ...." And he goes on to criticize his counterpart as a "bellaco, frión, y ladrón ...." He then describes Don Quixote in the most eloquent terms but, as usual, gets his words confused. At this point, Bowle inserts the following comment on Sancho's outburst: (161: 556-1; Part II) "*el matador de las doncellas*) O Sancho Panza Gracioso! El decir gracias no es para todos!" Bowle has become so enamored of Sancho that he literally bursts forth in mirth at Sancho's method of expression. In addition, he has incorporated the squire's statement from a few lines above into his very own.

A well-defined portrait of the character of Sancho has become complete for Bowle. The editor sees in him a living individual — a human being of feeling and warmth who emits the most ridiculously funny remarks and who is capable of strong emotion and sentiment. He is more than the foolish, sly creature pictured by earlier writers. The editor has raised Sancho to more dignified, even noble, heights.

The re-evaluation of the character of Don Quixote by Bowle occurs in much the same way except that he is much more effusive in those places where he permits himself some freedom of expression. Most of the remarks are like the following, which merely refers the reader to cases of similar actions elsewhere with no actual statement about the character himself: (141: 484-3) "*Lle-*

garonse á el, que libre, y seguro dormia, y le ataron muy bien las manos) El tratamiento del Cavallero aquí muy [sic] parece á estos pasos." [Quotations are then inserted from Pulci and Ariosto in which Orlando is treated like Don Quixote.]

What is said here presents nothing new regarding Bowle's approach to the novel and its characters. However, not all his statements are so noncommittal. In Part I, chapter XXIX, when the *Cura* comes out to greet Don Quixote, he mentions "la gran Compluto" in a very flowery speech. Bowle chooses this point to rhapsodize on Alcalá de Henares: (106: 283-8) ".... *O Alcala! Ciudad sobre todas las otras del mundo Famosa, y Dichosa* en aver producido tan ilustre Varon!"

This effervescent mood is precisely the one found in Part II, chapter LIX. Here where Avellaneda's work is being closely examined, Bowle delivers some of his most significant personal comments. The most important of them regarding a new feeling toward Don Quixote is expressed when Don Quixote declares that he will not go to Zaragoza. Bowle writes: (141: 465-8; Part II) "O Autor celeberrimo! O Don Quixote dichoso." Just as in the final comment concerning Sancho, he has stated so specifically and so very concisely what his feelings are toward the protagonist. Both of these utterances come toward the end of the book. They show a gradual involvement with the characters as the story — and Bowle's work with it — has progressed. Sancho becomes a real person for Bowle. Don Quixote becomes a living individual also, but, more than this, he is shown to have a deep integrity and feeling of fair play. He can sense the hurt inflicted by an imposter and reacts as any human being would. Yet, at the same time, Bowle realizes that behind the hero's actions there is a kind of calmness and majesty. He sees that Don Quixote does not act brazenly and rashly as he so often does. In this instance the hero, declining to be a part of that other knight's history, is portrayed with great dignity. In just a few words Bowle makes this all more pointed.

We find then that in 1781, although there is a faint glimpse of Don Quixote as a kind of spiritual figure, Bowle is still not ready to make such a far-reaching assertion. The roots of this idea are definitely here, nevertheless.

This chapter has dealt with Bowle's general attitude toward *Don Quixote* as a novel. Of necessity it has touched on several subjects because only in this way could any conclusions be drawn. The entire construction of the edition allows so little penetration on the editor's own part that we have to look underneath the surface to draw out the ideas present. The one comprehensive conclusion made is that Bowle sees the novel as something new, yet fitting into existing literary traditions. This is assumed from the enormous quantity of references he gives. From a very elementary standpoint the numerous quotations from Covarrubias, Aldrete, Nebrija, and Núñez show how Bowle finds that *Don Quixote* follows older currents of words, expressions, and proverbs. The use of the chivalric works — and closely related to them, the *romances* and the Italian epics — indicates that, within that genre which Cervantes was supposedly ridiculing, he continued its themes and more important, its language and style. Cervantes absorbed all the old forms as a foundation on which to construct his own work. These old forms permeate his novel so much that, if they were removed, the book would be hollow and of scant import.

With all Cervantes' adherence to preceding traditions, however, there is something new in his book. This is never stated forthrightly by the editor, but we sense it beneath his comments. When Bowle waxes most lyrical, we find that his admiration and love for the characters evoke intimations of new attitudes and interpretations. This is quite apparent in his vision of Sancho as a living human being who is at the same time logical, sensible, and sentimental. It is an attitude which, already developing in the eighteenth century, receives strong support from Bowle. A new attitude is even more apparent in his vision of Don Quixote. In the regally calm presence exhibited by the knight near the end of the novel, Bowle perceives the incipient notions of Don Quixote as a spiritual figure. For the editor, Don Quixote has finally left that world of rash decisions and reckless actions and very hesitantly has begun his way to becoming a symbol of the last bulwark against the enemies of all man's visions and hopes.

V

BOWLE'S GENERAL ATTITUDE TOWARD CERVANTES

At the end of the prologue to the *Anotaciones* there is a seven-page list entitled *Autores citados en las Anotaciones*. This catalogue, already noted in chapter III, presents us with an interesting subject: Bowle's belief about Cervantes' literary, artistic heritage. From the appearance of this list, Bowle obviously believed that Cervantes had a tremendous store of knowledge about significant and minor writers, including those from Homer up to 1600.

The list contains works of both writers of Antiquity and contemporaries of Cervantes. By so often citing these writers whom he knows so well, Bowle indicates that Cervantes was steeped in knowledge of them also. As a result, his edition of the novel turns out to be a kind of reference work showing parallels between other works and the novel under consideration. In so constructing his commentary, he leaves us with the problem of ascertaining exactly what concept he has of Cervantes' literary background. He gives us an early view of Cervantes as an avid reader and investigator of Western literature. This same view is widely held today, and also refuted. At the outset then we must strive to find out what Bowle's views are. The idea we must keep uppermost in mind is that Bowle believes that Cervantes knew all the works cited and that he must point out all of Cervantes' sources to show what a truly learned scholar his author was.

The books and authors listed by Bowle can be divided generally into three groups. The first comprises writers of the classical period — Virgil, Livy, Ovid, and others. The second is composed of those later writers who could conceivably have had some influence on Cervantes. Writers like Dante, Boccaccio, and Garcilaso, and works like *La Celestina,* the chivalric romances, and *La pícara Justina* go in this grouping. The third group, as set up here, has little to do with Cervantes directly because those authors included in it come after his death. People like John Talbot Dillon and Fray Martín Sarmiento belong here. Their works for the most part are reference books. Bowle himself is much more concerned with them obviously, since they provide him with material about Cervantes' life (Sarmiento) or about Spain in general (Dillon). In this part of the study only the first two groups concern us.

In presenting classical references, Bowle is not at all timid. The number of writers mentioned is impressive. Most often cited are Ovid and Virgil. This is to be expected since they were much better known by the general public. When Cervantes refers to geographical locations or to the characteristics of certain peoples or objects, Bowle presents selections from the *Aeneid* to show how similar descriptions are found in the Latin poem. In Part I, chapter XIV, Cervantes refers to Cerberus as the "portero infernal de los tres rostros" (52: 96-11). Bowle gives a short citation from the *Aeneid* explaining that Cervantes was referring to Cerberus. Immediately we have the desire to chastise Bowle for himself not explaining to what the text refers. It would be much more advantageous for the editor to inject his own views and not list only quotations from earlier writers. Yet such is not Bowle's method, and we soon take the work as it is, no longer wishing for more of the editor's personal comments. It then becomes easier to accept the numerous references to Virgil — whether they appear to have great significance at first or not. Very typical of most of the quotations from Virgil are ones like "*Flumina Thermodontis/* Pulsant, & pictis bellantur Amazones armis." (64: 134-19) or "Tria Virginis ora Dianae." (134: 453-30). The first is in explanation of the words "del claro Termodonte" and the second, of "Luminaria de las tres caras."

Fortunately many of the quotations from Virgil are quite relevant. In discussing how close the donkey and Rocinante are in Part II, XII, Cervantes called them another "Niso, y Eurialo"

(31: 84-28; Part II). Bowle quotes from the *Aeneid* showing how great was their friendship. Cervantes also called the two animals another "Pilades, y Orestes." Bowle cites a passage from Hyginus, indicating the closeness of these two ancient heroes. This kind of information is more pertinent and carries more weight when it is backed up by another author, especially one who is less known.

Two last instances show further uses which Bowle makes of Virgil. The references are much longer, and both concern events which are known to practically any reader. The first deals with the famous wooden horse used by the Greeks in the conquest of Troy, and the second concerns the story of Dido and Aeneas. Cervantes mentions the horse when discussing the adventures of Don Quixote and Sancho on Clavileño (II, XLI) (105-6: 312-2; Part II). About six lines are quoted from the *Aeneid* giving a description of the structure and what its purpose was. The temptation to criticize Bowle comes up again. Why does he not himself explain what all this means? But now we begin to realize that this is not his purpose — his own explanations would be of little value, or so he believes. What he is seeking is to place Cervantes and *Don Quixote* on a level heretofore not given them. By constantly proving the similarities between classical works and *Don Quixote*, he can place the latter on a level with the classics, which, to his eighteenth-century mind, is the height of honors. When he quotes about the Trojan horse or when he presents passages (II, LXXI) about Dido and Aeneas, we do not need to fuss over the uselessness of such references. To present the classical lovers' travails so late in the book when he has already made various mentions of them is not so ridiculous after all. Bowle believes that Cervantes is directly acquainted with everything cited here. It would be impossible to proclaim the *Quixote* a work deserving a place among the classics if its writer had no real knowledge of the ancient authors. With this thought prodding him on, Bowle eagerly includes sources which prove Cervantes' familiarity with all parts of classical works. There is no desire to degrade Cervantes by showing how unoriginal he was. It is rather the opposite: Cervantes merits praise and veneration precisely because he assimilated the works of Antiquity so well. Since we understand Bowle's attitude and his purpose behind the entire edition, we do not criticize. It is this lack of comprehension by several of Bowle's contemporaries that caused him to be maligned so severely. Had they tried to understand his motives better, they would have been less apt to treat him and his work so harshly.

The number of times Ovid appears is certainly as great, or greater, than that for Virgil. Many of these references also seem strained, but generally they have a more direct relation to the lines in the text. As would be expected, most of them explain mythological or somewhat fictionalized historical characters of Antiquity. In I, XIV, where Grisóstomo has written his famous lament, figures such as Tantalus and Sisyphus are called upon to mourn over the forlorn poet's state (51-52: 96-1). A long series of verses is given from the *Metamorphoses* telling specifically who these people were. Again (Part I, chapter XLIII) when Don Quixote addresses the sun proclaiming his jealousy because the latter may look fully on Dulcinea's countenance, he says he will be more envious than the sun himself was when he had to "correr por los llanos de Tesalia, o por las riberas de Peneo ...." Bowle assumes that Cervantes knew this incident well and presents those passages which show how wildly Phoebus went after Daphne. At this same place in his *Anotaciones* he gives a quotation from Pliny stating where all this took place ("Flumina *Thessaliae*, Apidanus, Phaenix, etc. Et ante cunctos claritate Peneus.") (135: 454-11).

There are similar clarifications as to who Phaethon, Actaeon, and Pyramus and Thisbe were. In Part II, chapter XLI (106: 313-19; Part II) Cervantes writes "mozo que quiso regir el carro del Sol su padre." Bowle cites Book II of the *Metamorphoses* telling how Phaethon begged his father to let him drive the chariot across the sky. In II, LVIII, when Don Quixote is so astonished on finding himself among several beautiful shepherdesses, he states that he is like "Acteon, quando vió al improviso bañarse en las aguas á Diana." Bowle quotes Ovid (Book III): "Per nemus ignotum non certis passibus errans/ Prevenit in lucum: sic illum fata ferebant./ Actaeon fugit Antoneius heros:/ Et se tam celerem cursu *miratur* in ipso." (138: 452-17; Part II). Then when the tale of Pyramus and Thisbe is mentioned, he says only that the myth can be found in Book IV and gives the pages of the edition he uses. For some reason, this incident does not merit the lengthy quotation given Dido and her lover (Part II, chapter XIX) (52: 142-30; Part II).

There are three instances where this kind of notation is of extreme value. All concern the legend of Perseus and are scattered about in both Parts of *Don Quixote*. In II, LXIV, Altisidora sings a song to the knight containing the lines: "Si te criaste en la Libia ... Si sierpes te dieron leche?" The lines are quite vague, and there is no other comment making them any clearer. Bowle sees that Cervantes is speaking of the Perseus myth, and he quotes from Book IV of the *Metamorphoses* about Perseus' victory over the Gorgons: "Cumque super Lybicas victor penderet arenas;/ Gorgonei capitis guttae cecidere cruentae:/ Quas humus excerptas varios animavit in *angues,*/ Unde frequens illa est infestaque terra *colubris.*" (111-112: 339-15; Part II). This clarification of a rather uncommon reference indicates the wide background of Bowle. The editor would have us infer that it indicates Cervantes' wide background also.

Part I, chapter XXXIII contains the story of *El curioso impertinente*. In it there is another reference to the myth of Perseus. This particular reference is rather ambiguous except to those who might have a good foundation in classical mythology. Lotario is lecturing Anselmo on the foolhardiness of his project. He quotes some lines from a play which he has seen: "Que si hay Danaes en el mundo,/ Ay pluvias de oro tambien." Bowle finds in the *Metamorphoses* (IV) the supposed origin of these lines for Cervantes: "Neque enim Jovis esse putabat/ Persea; quem pluvio Danae conceperat auro." (117: 327-9). The matter becomes clear when we remember that Perseus was born to Danaë after Jupiter (Jove) appeared to her in a shower of golden rain.

The final Ovidian reference mentioned here holds interest for reasons other than the clarification of the text. It occurs in relation to the incidents in I, XXV, when Don Quixote is to do penance in the Sierra Morena while Sancho carries a message to Dulcinea concerning his master's actions. Don Quixote tells him to mark his way so that he will be able to return easily, and he says to do so "á imitacion del laberinto de Perseo." Bowle finds a passage in Book IV of the *Metamorphoses* which could substantiate the lines of Cervantes: "Narrat Abantiades [Perseus — editor's note], gelido sub Atlante jacentem/ Esse locum, solide tutum munimine molis./ ——Se per abdita longe/ Deviaque, & silvis horrentia saxa fragosis/ Gorgoneas tetigisse domos." (96-97: 228-11). This is not too close to the text; there is no mention of a labyrinth or of a thread to be used as a guide. The temptation is strong to say that Cervantes confused the myths of Perseus and Theseus. The mention of a labyrinth and a thread certainly sounds more apropos of the tale of Theseus. Bowle himself senses this, but does not come out and boldly say so. His choice in wording is exquisite: "*Parece* [italics mine] aludir el Autor á estos versos de *Ovidio*." If Cervantes was really confused about the two ancient myths, and it seems that he was, [1] it is odd that Bowle does not comment on his author's mistake more emphatically. He does point out errors of Cervantes in one or two places, but his corrections are infrequent. Evidently, since he can find a vaguely similar Ovidian selection involving Perseus, he assumes that it is to this that Cervantes is referring. This would not be our manner of approaching the subject, for we would want to question the accuracy of Cervantes' statement. Yet again we are forgetting the editor's basic aim of ennobling the position of Cervantes and *Don Quixote*. His purposes include emending defects only when they are quite obvious. To suggest an error where he cannot be sure that there is one would be unnecessary and unworthy of his final goal.

Bowle cites many other classical writers, and, of these, a group composed principally of historians calls our attention next. Most of them are commonly known to modern readers: Suetonius, Sallust, and Pliny. Also less easily recognized individuals like Valerius Maximus and Hyginus can be included here. By relying on these writers, Bowle necessarily assumes a great acquaintance with classical authors on the part of Cervantes. It is not so dif-

---

[1] However, Rodríguez-Marín believes that Cervantes is not to blame: "Sabido es para cualquiera que haya saludado la mitología que fué *Teseo*, y no *Perseo*, quien con el hilo de Ariadna salió del famoso laberinto de Creta. ¿Por qué, pues, *Perseo* en la edición príncipe y en las otras dos de Cuesta, entre las más de las antiguas? ¿Acaso por ignorancia de Cervantes? Es de presumir que no...." (Rodríguez-Marín, in the notes of his edition of *Don Quixote*, Clásicos Castellanos, II (Madrid, [1961]), p. 320.)

ficult to accept Bowle's contention that Cervantes knew Virgil and Ovid well. However, to assume an equally sound knowledge of less renowned authors is a little risky.

Representative citations from Hyginus, Sallust, and Valerius Maximus, and most of those from Pliny are somewhat superficial and are much like those from Virgil. Hyginus has already been mentioned in connection with Virgil where Bowle notes the friendship of Rocinante and the donkey. When Cervantes mentions "laberinto" and "Teseo" in Part I, chapter XLVIII, Bowle cites several lines from Hyginus giving a succinct history of Theseus' stay on Crete (146: 504-13).

Don Quixote mentions the temple of Diana in Part II, chapter VIII, as one of the Seven Wonders of the Ancient World. Bowle cites Hyginus again as a basis for such a statement. He also gives a more lengthy passage from Valerius Maximus (22-23: 56-20; Part II). Neither of the quotations has anything to do specifically with the content of Don Quixote's speech as a whole, for both deal only with the reference to the temple. Bowle believes that the general content of his author's passage needs no further comment. All that is lacking is to indicate what the sources are for such a reference. The editor's attitude in these references is important because it points out again his approach to his subject. He is simply trying to give a firm basis for granting Cervantes a higher position of esteem. The desire to clarify vague passages with explanations and interpretations of his own never really becomes a part of his approach, therefore.

The one pertinent reference from Sallust and several from Pliny are similar to those discussed above. When Cardenio is telling his tale of woe in Part I, chapter XXVII, he breaks out in a series of recriminations against Fernando. Among other things he calls him "Catalina cruel." Bowle inserts a short note from Sallust showing exactly how terrible Catiline was: "Catilinae ab adolescentia bella intestina, coedes [sic], rapinae, discordia civilis, grata fuere." (101: 245-29).

There is a similar quotation from Pliny explaining who Mausolus was and how the word *mausoleum* originated (24: 59-5; Part II). Other citations from Pliny arouse the reader's curiosity in addition to clarifying vague passages in the novel. In Part I, chapter VI, when the books from Don Quixote's library are being burned, *Palmerín de Inglaterra* is saved and deemed worthy of being placed in a box like the one "que halló Alexandro en los despojos de Dario ...." Rather than discuss the importance of the decision, Bowle chooses to explain the reference to the "caja de Alexandro." In Pliny he finds the following unusual and intriguing note: "Alexander Magnus *inter spolia Darij* Persarum regis unguentorum *scrinio* [sic] capto quod erat *auro gemmisque ac margaritis preciosum,* varios ejus usus amicis demonstrantibus, imo Hercule, inquit, *librorum Homeri custodiae detur.*" (29: 35-21).

Two references from Pliny, mentioned here merely because of a certain amazement they cause, are indicative of some of the reference material in general. One wonders exactly how Bowle always finds rather erudite sources for such unusual expressions. When Don Quixote is lying quite awake in the inn before Maritornes' arrival (Part I, chapter XVI), he is described as having "ojos abiertos como liebre." Bowle supplies a quotation from Pliny agreeing with the statement: "*Patentibus oculis dormiunt lepores.*" (57: 115-19). The whole situation is a trifle ludicrous. To give such a source heightens the whole comic effect although this certainly is not the intention of the editor. The other incident concerns Part II, chapter X, when Don Quixote has great difficulty believing that it is Dulcinea coming toward him. He murmurs to Sancho: "podre señalar este dia con piedra blanca, ó con negra." From Pliny comes "O *diem laetum, notandumque mihi candidissimo calculo.*" (27: 69-8; Part II). After this there are references to Bartolomé Leonardo de Argensola and Juan de Mal Lara. The quotation from Mal Lara reads: "Los antiguos *señalavan el buen dia con piedra blanca.*" The citation from Pliny gives a much more learned basis to Cervantes' sentence, but the one from Mal Lara really explains what is meant more precisely.

Suetonius, Livy, and Lucius Florus are other historians who appear in the *Anotaciones*. There are many references to Suetonius especially, but one will show the type of commentary in general. In II, XXIV, Don Quixote talks of the importance of arms, and he says that death is not undesirable when it comes honorably. A sentence follows referring to a statement by Julius Caesar:

"Preguntaronle á Julio Cesar, qual era la mejor muerte, respondió que la impensada, la de repente, y no prevista." (67-68: 191-1; Part II). There is a very long selection from Suetonius to give the origin of Cervantes' statement. The interesting question is why Bowle should comment on this particular line because no commentary is necessary. In fact, some of the previous lines badly need explanation and are equally deserving of notice. The only reasonable answer is that Bowle, seeing such a fine source in Suetonius, grasps the opportunity to illustrate the learning of Cervantes. Certainly the line cannot merit such overlong treatment for any other conceivable reason.

The reference from Livy is similar in that the line for which it is provided is little deserving of much comment. However, Cervantes evidently made a slight error, and Bowle, as he rarely does, quietly points out the mistake. At the same time, what he says does not harm the image he is creating of his author. Basically Cervantes is correct, and his statement can still be based on the work of such a prominent writer as Livy. The incident takes place in Part I, chapter XIV, when Marcela appears and Ambrosio goes into a diatribe on her cruelty in appearing at this time. He refers to her as "la ingrata hija al de su padre Tarquino." Bowle says "Olvidóse aquí el Autor .... Alude sin duda al este hecho Historico. Amens Tullia [*la muger no la hija de Tarquino*] per patris [*Servij Tullij*] corpus carpentum egisse fertur." (52: 97-24). ² Cervantes is not actually criticized by the editor's reprimand. Bowle's obvious purpose of clarification is well-joined here to the less conspicuous one of exalting his author. Were the editor to emphasize the mistake, he would only detract from that prestige which he is seeking to give Cervantes.

There are just a few more ancient authors who must be noted because they complete the picture for the classical period. For the most part, they are cited less often than those previously mentioned. The quotations are of no great import except that

---

² "Tullia: In Roman legendary history... daughter of king Servius Tullius and wife of Tarquinius Superbus. She stirred her husband to oust her father from the throne, and when the latter had been murdered, drove her chariot over his dead body." *The Oxford Companion to Classical Literature*, (Oxford, 1940), p. 440.

they further develop the general view of Cervantes as a well-read student of Antiquity. Lucan is mentioned several times, but the references have little to do with the basic meaning of the lines of the text. The same is true of Martial and, to an extent, of Juvenal. The latter is quoted several times in maxim-like sayings. According to our editor, "nobleza consiste en la virtud" (Part I, chapter XXXVI) can be based on "Nobilitas sola est atque unica Virtus." (121: 373-19).

Even Plautus is cited — oddly enough, when Rocinante is being described in I, I: "que tantum pellis et ossa fuit." Bowle finds something similar in the *Aulularia* and decides that it is these lines which Cervantes had in mind: "M. Volo ex te scire qui sit agnus curio. E. *Qui ossa atque pellis totus est,* ita cura macet." (11: 5-8). A little more to the point is an allusion to the fable of Phaedrus about the frogs and the stick of wood. This concerns Don Quixote's letter of advice to Sancho while the latter is governor of Barataria (Part II, chapter LI) (123: 398-28; Part II).

Again, principally because of their names, Horace and Homer are mentioned. They are cited quite rarely, and most of the references to Horace state simply that an idea (or sentence) in *Don Quixote* is like one of his. In Part II, chapter III, Sansón Carrasco talks about jealous censors and says "aliquando bonus dormitat Homerus." Bowle refers us to the *Ars Poetica* (13: 25-22; Part II). Homer is cited when Don Quixote has the unfortunate battle with the sheep in Part I, chapter XVIII. One of the "armies" is supposed to be from the area of the "famoso Zanto." Bowle inserts a short quotation in Greek from the *Iliad* (63: 134-17).

The great acquaintance of Cervantes with the writers of Antiquity which Bowle has been showing implies good judgment, forthrightness, and good taste. Yet something is still lacking if the author does not have much knowledge about modern writers. Throughout the *Anotaciones* this second purpose of proving Cervantes' knowledge of the latter becomes increasingly evident to the reader simply through the accumulation of works and authors. Such well-known writers as Dante, Petrarch, Camoens, Juan de Mena, and surprisingly Chaucer and Geoffrey of Monmouth appear. Yet these writers are seldom referred to after they appear initially. They are not mentioned nearly so much as Covarrubias and certainly not so often as the romances of chivalry. The correlations between *Don Quixote* and numerous chivalric works are astounding, and in 1781 they must have been even more so because few of these similarities had really been proved before. By considering at length the correspondences with these books, Bowle does not leave his main purpose aside. In presenting the similarities, he is still portraying a very intelligent man through Cervantes' great interest in reading. At the same time, he succeeds in proving his author's knowledge of that literary genre which gave rise to *Don Quixote* in the first place.

Since the chivalric books are so prominent in the notes, we can begin with them to see Bowle's view of Cervantes as a student of modern literary production. Of all the works mentioned in this grouping, *Amadís de Gaula* is the most often cited. It is first used when Bowle explains who "Urganda la desconocida" was. Again we note that Bowle himself is not explaining, but is rather accumulating references which themselves explain. In such a case as this, Bowle's method is actually more effective: "Urganda se despidió dellos: y el Gigante y *Galaor* anduvieron su via. Y preguntando *Galaor* al gigante quien era tan sabida donzella, él contavale como era *Urganda la desconocida*, y que se llamava assi, porque muchas vezes se transformava y desconocia." (3: xiii—). The identification of Oriana is handled in the same way: "El rey Lisuarte traya consigo á Brisena su muger, y una hija que en ella ovo quando en *Denamarcha* morara, que *Oriana* avia nombre, la mas fermosa criatura que nunca se vió: tanto que esta fue la que *sin par se llamó*." (4: xvi-17).

Not all the references from *Amadís de Gaula* are pertinent. Unfortunately the majority of the quotations from the other romances do not add any essential information either. Most of the quotations from *Amadís de Grecia* indicate textual similarities. A line from Part I, chapter II, reads: "Caminó sin acontecerle cosa que de contar fuese." From *Amadís de Grecia* comes: "Fueron quinze dias sin que aventura les *viniesse que de contar sea*." (14: 9-5). This procedure is noted in the other most frequently quoted books of chivalry. In Part II, chapter VII, we find: "Quixote y Sancho se abrazaron." From *Belianís de Grecia*, Bowle selects: "Don Belianis abrazó a su Escudero con mucho plazer, como aquel, que en estremo le queria, que ningun Cavallero se hallava que tal escudero tuviesse: *Flerisalte* le beso las manos." (21: 51-25; Part II). The line "Aquí, aquí valerosos..." from Part I, chapter VII, is related to "Entonces Carlo Magno dixo *á grandes vozes:* Aquí Cs, que agora es tiempo de emplear vuestras fuerzas." *(Carlo Magno)* (32: 39-20). From *Espejo de caballerías* comes "El fiero Gigante dixo: Señor C, suplico que vuestro nombre me digays. El buen Renaldos dixo: *Sepas que me llaman Don Renaldos de Montalban.*" This is supplied for Cervantes' "sabed que yo me llamo Don Quixote..." from Part I, chapter VIII (36: 51-14). *Las sergas de Esplandián* and *Tirante el blanco* are similarly employed.

Next we turn to more "acceptable" literary productions. The first mentioned are Spanish authors, many of whom have been referred to before in dealing with other facets of Bowle's edition. Of all the Spanish authors, Cervantes praises Garcilaso most. Bowle never fails to point out this fact, and in instances where the allusion may not be clear enough, the editor states that it is Garcilaso to whom Cervantes is referring. In Part II, chapter VI, Cervantes writes "el gran Poeta castellano nuestro" and Bowle inserts in his *Anotaciones* after this line: "Garcilaso De La Vega." (20: 44-21; Part II). The editor provides the original lines from Garcilaso's poems when Cervantes quotes or paraphrases them, and he commends Cervantes highly for his lauding Garcilaso.

Fray Luis de León is referred to several times, but none of the citations is unusual or significant. Most are correlations between lines. The correlating of sentences is true for Juan de Mena also, who is not mentioned more than once or twice. Juan Luis Vives has two rather long quotations in the *Anotaciones* (144: 494-15, 17). They are supposedly to explain "fabulas que llaman Milesias" and "las fabulas Apologas" (Part I, chapter XLVII). They do define these two types of fictional work, but mainly they give Vives' somewhat disparaging opinions of the genres. There is actually little of relevance in them as far as the context of the lines in *Don Quixote* is concerned. The selections serve more to present a view of Vives.

Pedro de Rivadeneyra is quoted much more frequently than any of these. Usually the citations are to show the similarity of the texts. One is included here because it points out the closeness of Loyola's actions to those encountered in the books of chivalry and, in turn, to what goes on in *Don Quixote.* When we have concrete examples of this relationship, it is a little easier to understand the kinship between Loyola and Don Quixote proposed by earlier critics of the novel. When Don Quixote is to be made a true knight in Part I, chapter III, we read: "mañana en aquel dia me aveis de armar cavallero: esta noche en la capilla de este vu [sic] castillo velare las armas." From Rivadeneyra's *Vida de San Ignacio* comes: "Ignacio como huviesse leydo en sus Ls de Cas, que los Cs noveles solian *velar sus armas:* por imitar él como *C novel* de Christo aquel hecho cavalleresco *toda aquella noche,* parte en pie, y parte de rodillas estuvo *velando* delante de Imagen de nu [sic] Señora." (17: 14-7).

Works of varied significance in Peninsular literature are referred to at times. Of these, one of the most frequently mentioned is *Las Siete Partidas.* Usually it is employed to explain customs and practices appearing in *Don Quixote.* Part I, chapter XXX has the lines: "se hincó de rodillas ante ella, suplicandole le diese las manos...." From *Las Siete Partidas* comes "*Besar* deve el vasallo *la mano al* Señor, quando se faze su vasallo." (109: 291-30). In Part II, chapter LXXIII, Cervantes writes "mas galan que Mingo," and Bowle provides a quotation from the fifteenth-century work.

There are several references to *La Celestina,* but they are of little importance. Typical is the following note on textual similarity: Cervantes (I, V): "del pie que cojeaba" — *La Celestina:* "Bien sé *de que pie coxeas,* yo te sanaré." (28: 31-20).

The picaresque works are cited with some regularity, but probably the best known, *Lazarillo de Tormes,* is used merely to note the similarity in lines or in the expression of ideas. Of all these works, *Guzmán de Alfarache* is the most quoted. This is understandable when one sees that the quotations are regularly maxim-like sayings. Alemán's work is the most favorable for such treatment. In Part I, chapter XLIV, we find "el demonio, que no duerme." From Alemán, Bowle takes "El Demonio vela, y nunca se adormece." (136: 465-25). The closeness of expression in *Don Quixote* and *La Pícara Justina* is pointed out also. From the prologue material of *Don Quixote* comes "dandose una palmada en la frente." Bowle cites: "Doyme en la frente con *Palma*, para preguntar á mi memoria." (2: vii-26). One feels compelled again to question the validity of all these quotations. They are superficial and hardly help to explain the text. Nevertheless, we do have a large compilation of authors and works to adorn Cervantes' intellectual stature.

Two writers connected with the New World are mentioned. The first is Padre José de Acosta, who is quoted for a grammatical reason. Don Quixote says in Part II, chapter II, "Yo seguro" instead of "Yo aseguro." Bowle comments: "Asi impreso en sus *Novelas*. Ed Madrid. 1613... yo seguro que os la den de muy buena gana. Así *Acosta*. Indias...." (10: 14-28; Part II). Certainly this construction exists elsewhere, and why Bowle should choose Acosta is not entirely clear. Alonso de Ercilla y Zúñiga is cited in nearly the same way. Cervantes has "bolverme Cazique" in Part II, chapter XXXV. After a definition from Covarrubias, Bowle writes further: "Así *Al. de Ercilla* en la Araucana." (97: 280-27; Part II). This reference is a little more pertinent than the citation from Acosta, and the relation Bowle later makes between statements in *Don Quixote* and *La Araucana* is quite relevant. In Part II, chapter XLIV, there is the line "historia tan seca, y tan limitada, como esta de Don Quixote." Bowle quotes: "Aunque esta segunda parte de la Araucana no muestra el trabajo que me cuesta, toda via quien la leyere podrá considerar el que se habra pasado en escribir dos libros de materia tan aspera y de poca variedad: pues desde el principio hasta el fin no contiene *sino una mesma cosa*." (110-111: 331-16; Part II). This kind of correlation is significant in that it brings works together very rarely compared before.

The Italians are the most numerous of the authors quoted from outside Spain. As noted earlier, Dante and Petrarch are among these, but carry little real weight since they are only occasionally referred to, and then with scant relevance. Where Cervantes wrote (II, XIV) "Aurora, que ya por las puertas, y balcones del oriente," Bowle inserts this citation from the *Pur-*

gatorio: "La concubina di Titone antico/ Gia s'imbiancava *al balzo d'oriente.*" (38: 101-12; Part II). There is a sentence from Petrarch's *De Remedijs* reading roughly like Cervantes' "sola una cosa teene [sic] mala el sueño, y es que se parece á la muerte." (II, LXVIII). (155: 520-19; Part II). Boccaccio is employed for notes like the following: (Part I, Prologue) "Son tan Rozines como Rozinante" — "Tutti í suoi cavalli infino al piu *misero ronzino.*" (5-6: xx-22).

Most of the references to Italian writers are to later ones like Pulci or Boiardo, whose relations to Bowle and *Don Quixote* have already been examined to an extent. Boiardo is typically represented in this correlation: (I, II) "que algun enano hacía señal de su venida" — "Orlando verso il Pino se n'andava/ Ecco sopra una torre appare un *Nano,/* Che incontinente *un gran corno sonava.*" (15: 10-9). To add to Cervantes' "uno de los pecados, que mas á Dios ofende, es la ingratitud" (I, XXII), Bowle draws upon Pulci's *Morgante Maggiore:* "O Carlo Imperador, quanto sé ingrato!/ No sai tu quanto é in odio á Dio tal peccato?" (84: 1886-3). Quotations from Ariosto are similar in tone. Ariosto, more than the others, however, is used to explain chivalric heroes, especially those less well-known. In Part II, chapter I, Cervantes has "quien mas gallardo, y mas cortés que Rugero." Lines from Ariosto are used to clarify this somewhat shadowy personage: "Ruggier il *gagliardo* Cavaliero." (7: 9-28; Part II). (One can only wonder at this "clarification," nevertheless.)

The last work of Italian origin considered here is a collection of tales called the *Cento Novelle.* Bowle repeatedly goes to this work for the clarification of obscure facts or names as it is one of the few sources which rather consistently gives pertinent information.[3] It is noted here because Bowle believes that he

---

[3] The history of the *Cento Novelle* is quite difficult to trace. After checking many histories of Italian literature, it was felt that the most concise and relevant relation of the work's development is in an edition of the collection produced by Guido Biagi. In his introduction he says that Carlo Gualteruzzi's edition (1525) is the first. The stories, according to the latter (whom Biagi quotes), are "la più antica . . . . di tutte le cose in prosa volgare scritte che insino a questo dì sono alla su notizia pervenute." (p. xxiii). Biagi refers to Vincenzo Borghini, who made an edition of the work in 1572. Borghini says that the collection of stories is older than the *Decameron.* He

has found the origin of Sancho's tale about the goatherd in Part I, chapter XX, in this collection.[4] Such an assertion shows again that the editor has done much investigation. We shall not question whether his assertion is correct or not. It is useful to us in that it emphasizes Bowle's rather painstaking erudition: "Este cuento se halla en Le *Cento Novelle Antiche*." The editor then presents a long list of similarities between Sancho's tale and that in the *Cento Novelle*. (72: 155-21...).

Camoens is cited several times, but, as with so many of the better known authors, little of importance concerning the text of *Don Quixote* is found in the citation. A quotation from *Os Lusíadas* is given (along with some from Pulci and others) to show its similarity to Cervantes' line in the prologue material: "Rompí, corté, abollé, y dixe y hize." The reference from *Os Lusíadas* is strikingly close: "O de Luso arnez, couraza, & malha,/ Rompe, corta, desfaz, abolla, & talha." (4: xvi-3).

The last writers to be noted in this rather long discussion of modern authors and works come from England, oddly enough. They are even more intriguing when we consider who they are. Cervantes writes of Merlin in Part II, chapter XXIII: "dicen, que fue hijo del diablo, no fue sino que supo un punto más que el diablo." (62: 176-28; Part II). To explain who Merlin was and how he might fit such a description, Bowle goes to the *Historia Regum Britanniae* of Geoffrey of Monmouth for a long quotation which gives the background of Merlin. Bowle assumes that Cervantes was well enough acquainted with this work to be influenced to write the above line.

---

also opts for a group of authors as opposed to any one writer of the work. Biagi concludes his investigation with a study of Alessandro D'Ancona's ideas, which Biagi considers the most logical. D'Ancona "conclude per l'unità dell'autore e suppone che il libro potesse essere scritto tra il 1280 e il 90." (p. lii). (*Le Novelle Antiche*, Con una Introduzione sulla Storia Esterna del Testo del Novellino per Guido Biagi (Firenze, [n. d.]).)

[4] Rodríguez Marín says that the tale is of purely popular origin and that Cervantes did not have to take it from any known work. He relates how an old servant used to tell him this same story when he was a child except that, instead of "cabras," it was "pavos" which were ferried across the stream. (This information comes from Rodríguez-Marín's edition of *Don Quixote*, Clásicos Castellanos, I (Madrid, [1961]), p. 120.)

The other quotation is from Chaucer. Bowle implies that Cervantes and Chaucer were inspired in a common source. The episode is that of the famous ride on *Clavileño* (Part II, chapter XLI): "Como el famoso *Clavileño* retrahe mucho al *Cavallo de Bronce* de nuestro muy famoso Poeta, el *Eñio Ingles,* G. Chaucer... Que murió el año de 1400, no será fuera de proposito mostrarlo. El dueño del *cavallo de bronce* fue *Cambuscan, Rey de Tartaria*.... Es de inferirse de todas circumstancias, que entrambos *Poetas Chaucer, y Cervantes*... bevieron de una, y de la misma fuente; y por ventura hallaron la patraña en alguna Historia Arabiga...." (103: 308-7...; Part II).

A series of lines from Chaucer to show how similar the two tales are follows the above quotation and ends with: "Las principales semejanzas son aquí señaladas." Bowle most likely does not intend to show a reliance of Cervantes on Chaucer. What he actually does is to make an indirect relation between the two figures. This is similar to what occurred with Geoffrey of Monmouth and the *Cento Novelle*. To make such unexpected relations is interesting, especially when little of this sort of thing had been done before. In these three cases then, much more so than with the classical and the other modern authors, Bowle does more than simply enhance the stature of Cervantes. He branches out into new directions, seeing *Don Quixote* in relation to new subjects and fields.

In this entire section the purpose has been to show what Bowle's over-all attitude concerning Cervantes is. We have seen how Bowle accumulates a great number of references showing correlations between *Don Quixote* and previous works. Of the classical authors we find almost all represented — from the important to the very minor. At times the minor figures have more real relevance to the text than some of the more easily recognized writers. In addition to the writers of Antiquity, there is a considerable number of references to modern authors and works. Here too the more famous writers do not have as much importance in many cases as do writers who are less highly regarded now. With the more contemporary writers, Bowle deviates from his aims on a few occasions and gives references which, no matter how generous we are, have nothing to do with his text and serve only to provide a certain prestige and a respected name.

Finally, it becomes obvious that Bowle's reason for compiling all these minutiae is not only to show the sources for Cervantes' lines and ideas. This is merely the most apparent and most superficial purpose. Of course, Bowle has this very aim in mind, otherwise he would never have taken up such a project. But there is another reason which is less conspicuous at first. The editor believes that *Don Quixote* has not been permitted to assume the "hallowed" place which it deserves; the novel has been relegated too long to the comic and the bawdy. Bowle, living in a century when so many learned investigations are produced, decides to right the injustice. He will establish Cervantes once and for all as a true scholar by showing the tremendous amount of learning evidenced in *Don Quixote*. First he must point out the strong foundation in classical literature which Cervantes obviously (to Bowle) possessed. With this first, most important point established, he can proceed to round out the colossal figure he is erecting. If Cervantes is to be proved a great artist, Bowle must also give evidence of Cervantes' acquaintance with more contemporary writers and their works. With the completion of such a portrait, Cervantes will become worthy of that esteem heretofore afforded only to the classical writers and, of the moderns, to individuals like Dante or Petrarch.

The significant thing is that Cervantes does emerge precisely as one of these writers. In all fairness, this is not solely because of Bowle's efforts. However, by placing Cervantes boldly among the classical authors, there can hardly be any other result. To achieve this goal is Bowle's basic purpose. For this reason, Bowle composes the *Anotaciones* as he does, and this is why he does not include more ideas or opinions of his own.

As a result of all the material assembled here, one more point presents itself. Bowle sets before the public a problem which has perplexed scholars for a very long time. The argument has gone on ever since as to what was the extent of Cervantes' cultural background. On one side there are those who grant him many educational advantages, both formal and informal. Others say that he had little schooling of any kind. On both sides, all affirm that Cervantes had a rather extensive self-education. With Bowle the question is brought out in the open for the first time. In only one place does he actually mention any concrete ideas about the situation, however: "Son muy pocos los que saben la dilatada erudicion de *Cervantes*. Las Acotaciones de los Autores Clasicos mostrarán, que fue él cursado en las escuelas: no admitirá la mas minima duda, que halló *la caxa de Dario* en *Plinio*, y lo que dixo de *Horacio* Cocles de *Floro*, ó antes de *Livio*, y lo de *Julio Cesar* de *Suetonio*...." (Prólogo a las *Anotaciones*, p. ii).[5]

The attitude expressed here is obviously the one which permeates the entire edition. Bowle assumes necessarily that Cervantes was well acquainted with all writers of Antiquity. He believes that he knew modern literary figures also. The force of the editor's convictions is such that it dictates the very nature of his work. With such an impetus, it is only natural to expect that his assertion will considerably influence succeeding commentators. In Bowle we have then a very early (if not the earliest) and a very powerful advocate of Cervantes' great background in all departments of learning. By lodging Cervantes so firmly among the important classical and modern writers, Bowle is decidedly in that group of critics who proclaim a great knowledge of literature for the author of *Don Quixote*.

Besides obtaining Cervantes a place among the revered authors of Antiquity and their equals among the Moderns, Bowle gives Cervantes an even more curious position. With all of his lauding of *Don Quixote* and its author, Bowle goes beyond his intended hopes and portrays Cervantes as somewhat more extraordinary than he ever expected. The figure that inevitably emerges from these pages of notes is one of the eighteenth, and not the seventeenth, century. Cervantes — well-versed in various literatures, manipulating with dexterity the vast stores of knowledge he possessed, and observing his fellow man with a certain benign dignity — becomes none other than an ideal of the eighteenth-century scholarly gentleman. In Bowle's notes Cervantes is not the sick, life-weary prisoner who writes a faintly veiled

---

[5] Bowle says much the same thing in a more straightforward manner in one of his letters to Dr. Percy (this one is dated July 28, 1780, and is now in the manuscript collections of the British Museum Library): "Cervantes tis most certain was no superficial scholar, but intimately acquainted with antient as well as modern litterature [sic]."

autobiography. With Bowle, the Spanish author is the complete reverse. There is no hint of weakness, of resignation and weariness because of burdens too heavy to bear, or of any physical or spiritual fatigue at all. The vision of Cervantes in this 1781 work is one completely of the eighteenth century — and an English one at that. It is a Cervantes who is robust and fearless. He is a man of wit, humor, and an inescapable charm; a man serious, knowing, and wise. He is an educated man who intelligently displays a great learning achieved by an ever insatiable thirst for more knowledge. The figure emerges as one which is satisfactory only from the eighteneth-century viewpoint: majestic, calm, all-knowing — an "enlightened" figure.

Cervantes, as he is pictured here, is not an individual who associates easily with his fellow man. This sounds strange as it is the complete opposite of our general idea of Cervantes. The creator of Don Quixote and Sancho necessarily had to be a part of that world which he fabricated, for otherwise he could never have succeeded in his very real creations so well. Yet this aloof Cervantes in Bowle's work is not forcefully cut off from the world in which he moves. Rather he gives the impression of observing from the sidelines, taking in with all-seeing eyes what goes on around him. He moves among people watching them, smiling and nodding but never actually becoming a part of their world. This is an even greater indication of an eighteenth-century refurbishing of Cervantes. Were he to move about too much and too enthusiastically in his milieu, he would be derided. He must observe his world instead at a polite distance, marking its habits and its ways. Later, in his writings, he can enjoy what he has seen by reliving it all, but to enjoy it openly is forbidden.

Cervantes, with Bowle's prodding, becomes a kind of patriarchal figure also. A dignity is inherent in him, earned by years of productive labor. Carrying this metaphor even further, we can say that, to Bowle at least, Cervantes appears as some god who has wandered back to earth. From him emanates an air of quietness, of grandeur, and of worldly and spiritual wisdom. He is a sort of fountainhead from which all that is good in the world flows.

From statements and references in the *Anotaciones* employed up to this point in this study it would appear that Bowle never actually delves into the emotional side of Cervantes' character. In no instance yet mentioned has Bowle allowed himself to penetrate the exterior of Cervantes. The editor is prone to reticence when it comes to expressing his opinions about very personal aspects of Cervantes' nature, for his idea is that such license is unbecoming in a major work. But Bowle's enforced restraint in the edition does break down once or twice, and when it does we are more apt to see what his true ideas are in his vision of Cervantes.

One of those places where his candor does become evident is on page 141 in the notes for Part II. The particular comment concerns chapter LIX where a somewhat detailed analysis of certain events in Avellaneda's Part II is given. After a few pages of mild rebukes against Avellaneda, Don Quixote is asked to read some of the incidents to see exactly what they are about and to express his opinion on the manner in which the author develops the plot. We are told by Cervantes that Don Quixote will have no part of this and refuses to be bothered with the details: "de las cosas obscenas y torpes los pensamientos se han de apartar." For Don Quixote and, thus, for Cervantes, this delicacy may be the result of an angry jealousy. Bowle takes it all at face value at any rate and writes a most intriguing commentary: (141: 465-1; Part II) "Los mas torpes Adulterios, y Homicidios, hacen los sugetos de dos Cuentos, sin ningun proposito, ni moral, en este libro [Avellaneda's], tan justamente menoscabado de todos hombres de buen gusto. Caps. 15, 16, 17, 18, 19."

At last that longed-for eighteenth-century expression appears — *good taste*. Bowle, like any proper gentleman of his time, expects a certain propriety. Even though at times the bawdiest and most vulgar kind of humor may exude through the nice exterior, there must be, nevertheless, that correct surface. The term *good taste* represents all that is right and acceptable on this surface. Only those works exhibiting this characteristic can be worthy of serious consideration.

When he criticizes Avellaneda's work by saying that it should be disregarded by men of proper taste, Bowle is giving voice to several significant ideas. First he is saying that Cervantes' work is not like Avellaneda's, and therefore deserves the admiration of all well-intentioned readers. We are to infer that Cervantes' *Don Quixote* will be praised by "todos hombres de buen gusto." Second is the indirect statement that *Don Quixote* (Cervantes') exhibits good taste. This assertion is far-reaching as regards Cervantean criticism, in that it definitely causes Don Quixote to lose that old stigma of being nothing more than a doddering madman. Yet the idea which most intrigues us here is that, through the reversal of what he says about Avellaneda, Bowle declares that Cervantes exhibited good taste in the conception and execution of his work.

John Bowle, then, makes of Cervantes that good-natured, benign, *honnête homme* representative of his own century. In his letter to the *Gentleman's Magazine* in January, 1781, (Volume LI), he presents this basic viewpoint most concisely. Here he finally lowers all the barriers which hitherto have prevented a more intimate approach to Cervantes:

> This last account of himself [Cervantes' prologue to *Persiles y Sigismunda*], with every one of his writings, have confirmed me in my notion, that the goodness of the man was equal to the grandeur of the genius. Sure I am, that good-nature and candour, charity, humanity, and compassion, for the infirmities of man in his most abject state, and consequently an abhorrence of cruelty, persecution, and violence, the principal moral he seems to inculcate in his great work, were the glorious virtues and predominant good qualities of his soul, and must transmit his name to the latest ages with every eulogium, due to so exalted a character. (p. 24). [6]

The line "the goodness of the man was equal to the grandeur of the genius" is significant in the development of Bowle's thought and attitude. It is a strong endorsement of Cervantes as a man and as an artist. Up to this point Cervantes has been represented as a scholar, a portrayal which has contained little of a real human being. This portrayal has been one of a man coldly intent on his work. He has associated with his fellow men more to observe

---

[6] A similar reading is in Bowle's *A Letter to the Reverend Dr. Percy* (p. 48) which adds: "He [Cervantes] is therefore to be regarded as a citizen of the world, and all have an interest in him."

them than to share any labor or endeavor with them. Now in this one sentence all the preceding judgments have been amplified. No longer is Cervantes such a coldly distant individual, but a man full of "goodness" and kindness. These expected natural instincts, moreover, are now emphasized equally with the author's intellectual capacities.

In the *Anotaciones* Bowle is so concerned with Cervantes' artistic capabilities that he fails to emphasize the inherently human side of his subject. That he can outline this other half of his author's make-up so succinctly is indicative of his insight into Cervantes. In the *Anotaciones* Bowle embarks on a new method of analyzing *Don Quixote*. In his analysis he puts Cervantes on a level heretofere not attempted. Now in this quotation from the *Gentleman's Magazine* he establishes the good nature of Cervantes once and for all. The sweeping change in criticism of Cervantes occurring in these years is nowhere more obvious than in these few words. Bowle is at the forefront of a re-examination of the Spanish novelist. Within Bowle's work we are witnessing a tremendous refocusing of attitude. We have definitely come a long way from all those superficial interpretations of earlier years.

Bowle, in conclusion, has changed the appearance of Cervantes in many significant ways. Cervantes has become a classical scholar steeped in ancient and modern literatures. In assuming his new role, he has inherited many of the editor's own characteristics. He is easily portrayed as an eighteenth-century gentleman who spends much of his time in his library or who observes, at a distance, the life around him. He acquires that most basic of all eighteenth-century necessities — good taste. Cervantes has become the eighteenth-century *bonhomme* or *honnête homme,* call it what one may, and for a while he will play the role of the "enlightened creator." Bowle, more than any other critic, brings this phenomenon about and to understand Bowle — and to understand Cervantes in his critical history as writer — we must realize what is effected here.

This new vision of Cervantes will lose much of its eighteenth-century tone eventually. As this happens, the view of Cervantes as a very learned man will not be changed, however, but rather will grow as more and more critics affirm Bowle's assertions (as if they were their own ideas, it might be added). Thus, in his portrayal of Cervantes as a contemporary, Bowle affirms the capabilities of the Spanish novelist more than ever. And at the same time, Bowle shows indirectly his own rather strong influence on succeeding opinions concerning Cervantes — an influence seldom admitted by critics.

VI

THE INFLUENCE OF BOWLE ON LATER
CERVANTEAN CRITICISM (1780-1840)

To complete our view of Bowle, we shall deal with his influence on the immediately succeeding commentators of *Don Quixote*. Since his approach to the novel is so different, it is to be expected that he would exert some control over the direction that Cervantean criticism takes. There are several more editions of *Don Quixote* in the eighteenth century, and more continue to appear in the first quarter of the nineteenth century. In this very brief sketch we shall study the important ones up through the mid-1830's. It is then that Clemencín's detailed work is published. This is the most complete of all before that time, and its date provides a good concluding point, since it carries us through the high tide of Romanticism.

The matter of influences is in itself somewhat ambiguous. As in the second chapter of this book, where a very general idea was given of Cervantean criticism for nearly two hundred years, what will be attempted here is an overall view of the formats of these other editions. In their physical make-up there will be some indication as to how pervasive the influence of the Bowle edition is. We shall not expect to see exact duplicates of his work, nor shall we find his particular method adopted rigidly. We shall have to look for influences in statements made by the commentators, in the underlying tones of their approach, and in the particular subjects they choose to explain. In these less obvious characteristics we shall find that Bowle has indeed begun a method of investigation of Cervantes and *Don Quixote* that will never really cease.

With the Romantic School (and this term is used very loosely — principally to refer to the period of c. 1790-1840), the discussion of Cervantes and *Don Quixote* becomes ever more popular. The general commentary is more personal and, if it may be said, much more lyrical. The writers allow themselves great liberty in expressing their own opinions, and therefore they, as the writers, are always much more visible in their works. The approach is basically that of Vicente de los Ríos, only carried a little further, regarding the presence of the commentator. It would be fairer perhaps to say that this manner of judging *Don Quixote* is not entirely a contribution of the Romantics of the early nineteenth century because it has its origins in the last quarter of the eighteenth century. Beginning with Ríos, this approach continues in the investigations of Pellicer and Quintana, for example, who are the last significant critics to write about the novel in the eighteenth century. In their comments they mix personal reactions with the general procedures emanating from Bowle's edition. This includes great attention to detail, such as providing the meanings of words and the clarification of obscure passages and references. They do not discard the concept of a classical edition but merely combine what is essentially eighteenth century, best seen in Bowle, with a more direct and personal manner.

To get a better idea of how far this "new" and more individualistic outlook will go, we can look at two non-Spanish critics who write about *Don Quixote* in the first decade of the nineteenth century. Their viewpoints are indicative of a more "esoteric" approach as opposed to a more "classical" one. One of the critics is Swiss and the other, German. Neither is much interested in the sources of Cervantes or in the allusions he makes to other works. They are more preoccupied with what his work represents symbolically. In the concise statements contained in their literary histories the nucleus of most of the dominant attitudes toward *Don Quixote* from approximately 1800 on can be seen.

Sismondi in his *De La Littérature Du Midi de l'Europe* (Volume III) finds the true merit of the novel in its ethereal import:

> L'invention fondamentale de Don Quichotte, c'est le contraste éternel entre l'esprit poétique et celui de la prose. L'imagination, la sensibilité, toutes les qualités généreuses tendent á [sic] l'exaltation de don Quichotte.... Ce dévouement continuel de l'héroïsme, ces illusions de la vertu, sont ce que l'histoire du genre humain nous présente de plus noble et de plus touchant; c'est le thème de la haute poésie, qui n'est autre chose que le culte des sentimens [sic] désintéressés. Mais le même caractère qui est admirable, pris d'un point de vue élevé, est risible, considéré de la terre.... (pp. 341-342).

Sismondi, who is influenced by the German Romantics, sees Don Quixote as the personification of all that is noble and beautiful in man. He is "la poésie" which struggles against all that is base in the world, "la prose." This tendency to elevate the knight into a kind of supernatural being — into a symbol, as it were — has definitely gained great impetus by 1800.

Bouterwek has more or less the same ideas, but he does not permit himself the lyricism which seems to pervade Sismondi's judgments so completely:

> It has often been said, though the opinion has, perhaps, not been fully weighed, nor even expressed with sufficient precision, that the venerable knight of La Mancha is the immortal representative of all men of exalted imagination, who carry the noblest enthusiasm to a pitch of folly; because with understandings in other respects sound, they are unable to resist the fascinating power of a self-deception, by which they are induced to regard themselves as beings of a superior order. (*History of Spanish and Portuguese Literature*, trans. Thomasina Ross, I (London, 1823), p. 333).

These views are presented to show more clearly the positions being advanced by new critics. Their ideas are not what is found in Bowle's edition of *Don Quixote* at all. Even in his most lyrical outbursts Bowle does not make such forthright declarations. We can, therefore, hardly expect the influence he exerts to be of this type. We shall find his influence in that kind of diligent investigation of the more obvious characteristics of *Don Quixote*. Although Bowle was so openly criticized when his edition appeared, it is interesting to see how greatly his work guides succeeding commentators. As some of the later editors fail to give Bowle proper credit, it is all the more satisfying to find that, through his influence on these works, he takes revenge on his tormentors.

Pellicer's [1] edition of *Don Quixote* appeared in 1797. Having worked with the novel and investigated many facets of it for a number of years, Pellicer presents the public with five volumes of his discoveries. He too believes that the novel is in need of commentary (notas "... historicas, otras literarias, otras morales, y otras tal vez gramaticales y criticas," Volume I, p. ix). Basically the pattern he uses is that established by Bowle. The difference is that his notes are at the bottom of each page of the text instead of at the end of the novel.

Near the beginning of his edition, when he is giving a brief résumé of other similar endeavors, he delivers a condescending opinion of Bowle's work: "... intentó una empresa, que, aunque superior á las fuerzas de un estrangero, siempre es loable.... pero como el anotador no escribia principalmente para los lectores españoles, se hallan muchisimas más utiles y necesarias para los estrangeros, que para aquellos. *No negaré sin embargo, que me he servido de algunas* [italics mine]." (Volume I, p. xvi).

The last statement is most important because Pellicer does not state the truth too exactly here. Not only does he use "algunas [notas]" which he acknowledges, he also employs many more of Bowle's notes for which he gives no credit to the English editor. In discussing the history of early editions of *Don Quixote* he follows explicitly what Bowle says and mentions the real first edition recorded by Bowle. Pellicer does no more investigating of his own and is content with copying Bowle's statement (Volume I, pages xcvi-xcvii). He says that Cervantes in the 1608 edition corrected some errors of the previous editions. He goes on to give seven examples of these changes — each one of which is in Bowle's *Varias Lecciones*.

Bowle explains passages by quoting from other works. Pellicer usually explains the passage himself, and seldom quotes from other

---

[1] The reader is referred to the bibliography for the exact dates and other specific information about the editions discussed in this chapter.

sources. But the correlation between the two editors is still evident and can be seen best in the impetus which Bowle's manner gives to Pellicer's work. This is obvious in those places where he uses the same or very similar quotations. In the poem to Rocinante in the poetic material at the beginning of Part I of *Don Quixote*, when Rocinante speaks of events in *Lazarillo*, Bowle provides quotations from the picaresque novel explaining the reference (5: xviii-9). Pellicer explains what took place when Lazarillo, traveling with the blindman, drank the wine with a straw. The guiding hand of Bowle can be seen merely in the fact that Pellicer finds a comment necessary here. The note concerning "pellis et ossa fuit" (ll: 5-8), which Bowle finds in Plautus, is handled in a slightly different way by Pellicer (Volume I, page 9). He first gives a long paragraph on the owner of the horse, Pedro Gonela. This is good; but then at the very end, he quite timidly inserts the quotation from Plautus provided by Bowle. No mention is made of the latter, however.

Bowle diligently searches out the source of Sancho's tale in chapter XXII about the ferrying of the goats across the stream. Pellicer says that the story is not original with Cervantes; however, he fails to say how he himself comes across this fact. Again, it must be through the 1781 edition, for the following note sounds very much like Bowle (72: 155-21): "*Pasage de las cabras.* Este cuento no es á la verdad original de Cervantes, pues aunque le varió y mejoró tanto, que le hizo suyo, tomó la sustancia de otro que se lee en *Le Cento Novelle antike* [sic], que se hallan al fin de *Cento Novelle scelte* publicadas en Venezia año de 1571...." (Volume II, p. 87).

Pellicer presents a synopsis of the story; but, unlike Bowle's quotation, which is in the original Italian, Pellicer's is in Spanish. This denotes a basic difference between the two editions — Bowle keeps the Italian in order to stress Cervantes' learning. This idea does not concern Pellicer.

In Part II, chapter III, Sansón Carrasco enumerates certain faults that readers have found in *Don Quixote* (Part I). Among them is Cervantes' "failure" to say "quién fue el ladron que hurtó el rucio á Sancho, que alli no se declara...." Pellicer writes: "Este pasage es uno de los que prueba que Cervantes no revio su obra, *segun han observado algunos* [italics mine]; pues en los lugares de la Parte I, que es la censurada aquí por Sanson Carrasco, dice que el ladron que robó el asno á Sancho Panza, fue Gines ó Ginesillo de Pasamonte...." (Volume IV, p. 34). One of those "algunos" is Bowle: "Parece el autor aquí aver olvidado las mutaciones del Texto...." (13: 26-3; Part II).

There are many similar incidents. In Volume V, page 65, of his edition, Pellicer gives the origin of the incident of the old men who come to Sancho Panza (who is now Governor of Barataria) seeking justice. One of the men claims to have paid up the debt which has caused the argument. He actually does pay it, handing over the money inside his staff. Pellicer says that the story comes from Jacobus de Voragine. This same source is found in Bowle, with the quotation in Latin. (The name of the story is also given — *De Sancto Nicolao*.) (Bowle: 113: 345-13; Part II).

One last quotation is given in which Pellicer refers to Bowle. He does so to criticize what the latter writes rather than to praise or to admit that what Bowle proposes is worthy of consideration. It concerns the Clavileño episode previously discussed. Most of the comment is included because it shows so well Pellicer's general attitude toward Bowle. Pellicer is quite willing to accept nearly all that Bowle discovers, but at times he does not follow the latter's guiding light for fear of being openly criticized because of his heavy reliance on the earlier commentary. The episode is in Part II, chapter XLI (Bowle: 103: 308-7 on; Part II):

> D. Juan Bowle en sus *Anotaciones á Don Quixote:* p. 103. dice que G. Chaucer... habla de otro caballo muy semejante al Clavileño, solo que era de bronce. Era de Cambuscan, Rey de Tartaria.... Añade el señor Bowle que puede inferirse que asi Chaucer, como Cervantes bebieron esta patraña en una misma fuente, y que acaso la hallaron en alguna historia arabiga. Pero prescindiendo de si la del poeta ingles es invencion propia ó agena, la de Cervantes esta adoptada seguramente de la *Historia de la Linda Magalona hija del Rey de Napoles, y de Pierres, hijo del Conde de Provenza* impresa en Sevilla año de 1533.... Lo que solo se infiere es la semejanza que se advierte entre estos dos caballos; asi como pudiera tambien inferirse la que segun la hablilla antigua tenia con Clavileño en no comer ni dormir la mula de Iñigo Ezquerra, ó el Zurdo, á quien procreó su padre en un

espiritu malo en figura de una muger bien parecida, como se lee en nuestros genealogistas.... (Volume V, p. 4).

Bowle's comparison certainly is open to question. Yet Pellicer goes beyond mild criticism and indulges in the kind of smoldering sarcasm which may be seen in the last lines. This is unnecessary unless the writer feels himself at fault for too great a reliance on Bowle. Such is most likely the case here, for Pellicer can easily take advantage of this one instance to purge himself of guilt for his earlier heavy dependence on Bowle.

Pellicer's edition, as a whole, is significant in the development of Cervantean criticism in the eighteenth century. It is the next large edition after Bowle's work, but, as a contribution to this criticism, it is not so important as Bowle's endeavors. Many of Pellicer's notes are interesting, but they are often superfluous and irrelevant. References to the conditions of the poorer classes in Cervantes' time, or to the habits of criminal *ciegos,* or to the effects that the reselling of food had on the people's health are all entertaining reading; however, their place in a commentary specifically on *Don Quixote* is questionable. This tendency to ramble on and on is much too evident; it wearies the reader after a while no matter how intriguing the material may be.

Pellicer uses a method which is a combination of the procedures of both Ríos' and Bowle's methods. He is led by Ríos in his personal meanderings through what he finds in *Don Quixote*. In his attention to the meanings of words and to the location of source materials he definitely follows the pattern established by Bowle. Unfortunately Pellicer is not quite the honest critic he should be, and in innumerable instances he fails to give credit to Bowle where it is due. This lack of courtesy may be due to an unconscious imbibing in great part of Bowle's findings. Nevertheless, the rather sarcastic criticism he writes at times about Bowle shows that he is guiltily aware of his debt.

At the time Pellicer's edition appears, another is also published in six small volumes (three in 1797 and three more in 1798). At the front of the first volume is a "Noticia de la vida y de las obras de Cervantes" by Manuel José Quintana. It has no resemblance to Bowle's or Pellicer's editions, for it is only a short essay commenting on the salient facts of Cervantes' life and work as

Quintana sees them. Some of his thoughts are the tried and true ones of earlier years. He continues to hold the belief that Cervantes' principal aim was to banish the books of chivalry. Quintana does not wish to prove the worth of Cervantes by accumulating reams of facts as Bowle does. Nor does he wish to make useless personal statements which have no real connection with his subject. His work is like a small jewel in many respects, resting snugly among more pretentious investigations, but secure in its own intrinsic worth.

His brief investigation occupies a rather singular position at this stage of Cervantean criticism. The one basic theme which he expounds has much importance to us because it relates directly back to John Bowle. When Quintana was mentioned in the second chapter of this book, it was noted that in his praise of Cervantes he observes something rather new about the author's artistic endowments. Quintana believes that Cervantes' creation of his unique novel makes him comparable to Homer. He finds in Cervantes a person who stands much above his contemporaries ("... quando se compara ... á Cervántes con los hombres que le rodeaban, la obra parece un portento, y Cervantes un coloso." pp. xx-xxi). This is a strong statement in the novelist's behalf and is more profound than any of the verbose assertions of either Ríos or Pellicer. In all their grand pronouncements neither of these succeeds in capturing so neatly the growing awareness of the essential merit of Cervantes. By putting Cervantes on an equal footing with Homer, and in turn with all the significant writers of Antiquity, Quintana does exactly the same thing as Bowle, but with less effort than the Englishman. In reading Quintana's interpretation of Cervantes, one wonders exactly how great the influence of Bowle was in determining Quintana's attitudes. Quintana never says anything openly about the English editor, but in one place he makes a comment of particular import. The following quotation shows that he is familiar with Bowle's purposes (as not all of Bowle's contemporaries are) and that he realizes the importance of what Bowle is doing. Developing his familiar theme, he writes:

> Quando se ha comparado el Quixote con la Iliada no se advirtió que la comparacion era inaplicable entre dos

obras tan diferentes.... Pero si con mentar al padre de la poesía [Homero] se quisiese decir, que para escribir este libro se necesitaba tanta fuerza de espíritu como para componer la Iliada; de acuerdo entonces sobre ello añadiríamos que esa es una relacion que tiene Cervantes no solo con Homero sino con Sófocles, Virgilio, Taso, Corneille, Racine, y todos los grandes escritores. (p. xxii).

(Then in a footnote to this statement he writes:)

Otro punto de semejanza: sin embargo de ser un libro tan moderno, y á pesar del discreto prólogo que su autor le puso, se publica el Quixote á fines del siglo xvIII con un amplio comentario. Era preciso sin duda que pasase por las pruebas y vicisitudes de todas las obras clásicas. (pp. xxii-xxiii).

The last paragraph is obviously a reference to Bowle. Quintana, unlike Pellicer, grasps the underlying significance of Bowle's work. In just a few words he recapitulates the latter's intentions and gives Cervantean criticism a clearer sense of direction than it has had since 1781. Although he understands Bowle's purposes and may even use them as a basis for his own statements, he does not find it necessary to "re-do" Bowle's work as Pellicer does, in essence, adding superfluous material at the same time. It is fitting that eighteenth-century criticism in Spain should end on such a sane note. It summarizes the best of what that century produces regarding Cervantes.

For some reason the truly outstanding works on *Don Quixote* and Cervantes in the nineteenth century do not begin appearing until approximately 1820. There is scholarly work before this, of course, but that which interests us for its significant commentary is not published until this time. There is an edition of *Don Quixote* in 1832 in four volumes. Two years later two separate volumes are printed by the same publisher. They can be considered a part of this edition, although they are not always catalogued as such. The so-called fifth volume contains Ríos' *Análisis* and Navarrete's *Vida De Miguel De Cervantes Saavedra*. (Navarrete's essay was written several years earlier, and was first published around 1820. We study it here since it falls better into a closely knit group.) The sixth volume is composed of Bastús y Carrera's

Nuevas Anotaciones Al Ingenioso Hidalgo D. Quijote De La Mancha ....

Although it is longer and contains more concrete facts, Navarrete's essay is much like Quintana's in its form and approach. Navarrete recognizes the value of Bowle's edition and singles him out from all the noteworthy English investigators of the eighteenth century as most deserving of recognition: "Los ingleses, constantemente apasionados á Cervantes, y dignos apreciadores de su obra, no sólo tienen desde el año 1620 diez traductores de ella ... sino un comentador tan diligente y erudito como el doctor Juan Bowle." (p. 240).

Navarrete constantly refers to Bowle with remarks like "segun la oportuna observacion del doctor Bowle." (p. 257). When speaking of Pellicer, he says that he goes much too far afield in his notes and even forgets what his subject is (pages 277-278). He criticizes him also for his close dependence on Bowle. When Navarrete discusses the first editions of Part I, he notes Bowle's very early reference to what turns out to be the true first edition: "El Sr. Bowle ya dijo despues de citar la anterior [the real second edition which Navarrete still considers the first]: *consta que hubo otra del mismo año, lugar y forma;* pero Pellicer aunque citó esta noticia no pudo asegurarse de su certidumbre." (p. 443).

In general, Navarrete, while not producing an edition of the novel and commentary for it of his own, is quick to recognize the worth of the endeavors of others. Although he does not carry Bowle's precepts as far as Quintana, he notes the intent of the editor and lauds him in his efforts. In addition to recognizing Bowle's merits and without evidencing any feelings of prejudice, he acknowledges the significance of all English investigations of Cervantes during the eighteenth century. His statements are indicative of a healthier environment which Cervantean criticism now enters. In very broad terms, this criticism is more profound, less sarcastic, and less chauvinistic: "Asi fue como el empeño y estimulo de una nacion estraña despertó entre nosotros en aquel tiempo el recuerdo y la estimacion hacia el ingenioso autor del Quijote, divulgando por toda la Europa el mérito de aquella obra inmortal...." (p. 265).

In its organization, the volume containing Bastús y Carrera's *Anotaciones* resembles Bowle's notes very closely. It is not nearly so complete or "classical" a production, but Bastús follows Cervantes' text line by line, making comments of his own and also quoting from other sources. Among the commentators since Bowle up to this time, he is the one who most discusses the meanings of words and expressions. His avowed purpose is to show how close *Don Quixote* is to the works of chivalry, and he states that he will refer to them and quote from them liberally. The commentary is interesting because it contains résumés of the best known chivalric romances and gives little known facts about incidents and characters in them. It is, therefore, like a small encyclopedia regarding the books of chivalry.

By discussing words and expressions Bastús follows Bowle's precepts quite closely, and undoubtedly he is influenced by the latter in the manner of his approach. It is rather ironic to see that now, some fifty years later, Bowle's methods are instinctively imitated. Whereas his voluminous exposition of all this matter was criticized as silly and unnecessary in the 1780's, by the 1830's it is considered an essential part of any respectable commentary on the novel.

It is only natural that the parts which Bastús chooses to discuss are also found in Bowle's edition. For his explanation of "Termino ultramarino" (Part I, chapter VI) (30: 36-7), he uses nearly the same wording (and evidently the same source) as Bowle: "El que se concede para la prueba, proporcionado á la distancia donde se ha de hacer á diferencia del legal de ochenta dias." (Tomo I, Part I, page 45).

When Bowle gives the quotation about the temple of Diana (22: 56-20; Part II), he does not explain what occurs in the novel, but instead gives a description of what the temple was like. The passage itself is worthy of some more pertinent comment and, while we would not expect a personal note necessarily from Bowle, we might conceivably expect one from Bastús. Yet the latter has no comment of his own here (Tomo III, Part II, page 31). In fact, his treatment of the incident only shows more obviously than ever his great debt to the earlier editor. Although he does not quote Valerius Maximus, he describes the temple at length. An explanation of the classical reference is still thought to be more important than a clarification of the passage itself. One difference between the two commentators is that Bastús is much more personal because he uses his own words. The effect is, however, the same.

Of all these investigators of *Don Quixote* who come after Bowle, none follows his precepts so well as Bastús. In his method and in his choice of what to discuss, he clearly shows the influence of Bowle at all times. By this time it is not so much a conscious effort to imitate Bowle (as with Pellicer, who tries to cover up this dependence) as it is an unconscious imbibing of the organization, materials, and outlook inherited from the 1781 edition. By the 1830's, an acquaintance with this work has been generally disseminated enough so that the new commentators are not always aware that their approach and their comments are not actually their very own.

The last commentary to be considered in this brief analysis is Clemencín's,[2] which appears in six volumes from 1833 to 1839. It is the most thorough of the analyses of *Don Quixote* to this time. With its combination of Bowle's method and the judicious remarks of the editor, truly modern research into Cervantes arrives. It is the editor's use of Bowle's precepts which interests us here, for he is well aware of the merits of Bowle's edition. The passage of time has mellowed the acrimonious atmosphere existing in 1781, and, as a result, Clemencín can admire the work of the Englishman. This does not prevent him, however, from speaking of it in several places with a kind of benevolent tolerance. Clemencín appears to be clearly aware of his own talents. He can afford to look at earlier, and thus more primitive, accomplishments with a kind disposition:

> D. Juan Bowle, distinguido literato inglés, imprimió el año 1781 una nueva edicion del *Quijote* con un tomo de índices y otro de anotaciones, en que señaló las refe-

---

[2] Diego Clemencín (1765-1834), a member of various learned societies, was *Ministro de Ultramar* and of *Gobernación* in 1822. Under Isabel he again participated actively in the government. He wrote several erudite works, of which his edition of *Don Quixote* is the most valuable.

réncias á los autores latinos, italianos y caballerescos, y procuró explicar las voces que podian ser obscuras para sus compatriotas.... es mui digno de alabanza, y mui de admirar en un extrangero el conocimiento de libros castellanos con que enriquece y autoriza sus notas. Pero estas no alcanzan á auxiliar á los españoles en los puntos peculiares de sus costumbres y del idioma familiar, cuya perfecta inteligéncia en todas lénguas, y singularmente en la castellana, es imposible que adquieran los extraños... [Bowle] no trató jamás de hacer ninguna observacion crítica ni de juzgar del mérito ni demérito de la fábula. Sus anotaciones presentan el aspecto de una erudicion laboriosa, pero seca y descarnada: son como un almacén donde se hallan hacinadas mercancias de todas clases, unas de mayor y otras de menor precio.... (Volume I, pp. xxxv-xxxvi).

[Bowle] como extrangero, no alcanzó la fuerza del idioma, cosa siempre difícil, y á veces imposible.... (Volume II, p. 345).

As we have seen in our analysis of Bowle's edition, the general tone of Clemencín's statements is completely justified. Of all the more unfavorable opinions expressed about the edition, his are the least sarcastic. Like most commentators up to this time, however, he judges Bowle on a basis which is unfair. Clemencín, who is not approaching Cervantes with the idea of putting him on a level with the classical authors, fails to see Bowle's underlying purpose of elevating the novelist. Nevertheless, he does grasp the value of Bowle's work and uses a great deal of what Bowle writes. And this borrowing of Bowle's findings is the most curious note concerning Clemencín (and, indeed, all the commentators). In spite of all his criticism of Bowle because of his failure to understand the fine points of Spanish and because of his omnipresent definitions of words and phrases, Clemencín provides innumerable definitions and explanations of stylistic idiosyncracies. This particular criticism of Bowle by Clemencín and others becomes ever more untenable, therefore. Clemencín cannot really be justified in his reproaches of the eighteenth-century editor if he, in essence, does no differently. It causes us to question the entire credibility of the Spanish editors, who, on the one hand, say that no such explanations are necessary and then proceed to employ the very same method they criticize. Here once more, the influence of Bowle has so completely permeated the manner of editing *Don Quixote* that the editors themselves no longer quite realize the great discrepancies between what they say and what they do.

In the same vein, one questions the honesty of the following statement: "En resolucion, el *Ingenioso Hidalgo D. Quijote de la Mancha* carece hasta ahora de un comentario seguido y completo, como lo reclama su calidad de libro clásico...." (Volume I, p. xxxii). Bluntly, Clemencín is passing over Bowle's edition too easily. His statement naturally follows the previous quotations, but he sets himself up on too high a pedestal, forgetting how indebted he is to the first real commentator. We shall find that the distance between the two is not actually so great after all.

The principal difference between Bowle and Clemencín is that the latter explains things more fully. He, like most of those after Bowle, gives far fewer quotations, and these are used to substantiate his own ideas rather than to show the erudition of Cervantes. When he presents the meanings of words for which he criticizes Bowle so openly, he says the same thing as the latter, only with more words (the discussion of "yantaria" — 16: 12-18 in Bowle; Volume I, page 38, of Clemencín — is typical). Evidently he can easily forget his criticism of Bowle when he needs to.

When he comments on Don Quixote's modesty in not undressing, Clemencín employs words very reminiscent of Bowle's (111: 334-27; Part II): "Aquí contraviene Don Quijote á la antigua usanza de los caballeros andantes, tal como él mismo la describe en el capítulo 50 de la primera parte." (Volume V, page 375). The following sentence concerning Aeneas and Dido (Part II, chapter XLVIII; Bowle: 117: 367-29; Part II) shows how well he has assimilated the material in Bowle's edition: "Bowle cópia algunos versos de Virgilio y Ariosto, que mencionan este pasage de Eneas y Dido." (Volume V, page 460). Clemencín actually says nothing here, and the reference to Bowle is unnecessary. There is no justification for it unless he feels a need to compensate Bowle for the way he slights him elsewhere.

Indeed, many of the quarrels he gets into with Bowle are petty. In Part I, chapter VIII, where Bowle quotes from Covarrubias on "haciendo mas cruces" (36: 51-8), Clemencín has this to say: "Las cruces que se hacian los frailes, no eran de admiracion, segun entendió Bowle, sino de miedo, como indica la expresion misma: *siguieron su camino, haciéndose mas cruces que si llevaran al diablo á las espaldas.* Del diablo no se dice que es admirable sino temible." (Volume I, page 185).

He criticizes Bowle for comparing Chaucer and Cervantes in the Clavileño episode: "mas á pesar de la opinion de Bowle [103: 308-7; Part II], es evidente por su mismo contexto, que la idea principal de esta aventura de Don Quijote se tomó de la *Historia de la linda Magalona*...." (Volume V, page 307).

For all his faultfinding with Bowle, Clemencín has his own glaring problems which can be more irritating by far than anything in the Englishman's work. One reason for this is the recurrence of these "faults." For example, he is constantly berating Cervantes because of the novelist's style. Clemencín's own emendations are hardly better, and there is little necessity for them. The passage below indicates how useless these explanations and corrections are (in the quantities that he supplies them, at any rate): (Part II, chapter XXV: when speaking about the monkey's not explaining questions concerning the future) *"No responde á lo por venir.* Esto es, *no responde á las preguntas sobre lo por venir."* (Volume V, p. 33).

Cervantes' sentence is quite clear and absolutely no further comment is needed by Clemencín. The intent of Clemencín's comment — and there are many more like this — is no different from that of Bowle's explanation of words and phrases. It is impossible to accept Clemencín's notes here when elsewhere he criticizes Bowle for his unnecessary definitions of words.

Just as ridiculous are further comments on Cervantes' style. The quotation below concerning Cervantes' way of writing allows us to observe the "profundity" which Clemencín reaches at times. This explanation, like so many others, is not wanted and tends to diminish the image which Clemencín should project: (Part I, chapter XX) *"como villano ruin que sois./* Tres veces se repite el *como* en breve espacio causando un efecto desapacible: *Como es verdad que no los he visto en mi vida, como vos los habreis visto, como villano ruin que sois."* (Volume II, p. 139).

From what we have been saying, the impression may be given that we are trying to tear down what Clemencín has done. This is not our intention at all. It is simply feared that many readers of his edition who might not be familiar with Bowle's would tend to follow his statements too carefully and condemn the latter without cause. We have wanted to show that Clemencín falls victim to the same, or worse, vices in his notes without realizing what he is doing. He also forgets the importance of Bowle in relation to his own edition. This importance lies merely in the fact that it is Bowle who for the first time identifies so many of the sources utilized by Clemencín. This is seen more and more in such notes as the following. It is almost certain that if the same material were not found in Bowle's edition, little regard would be given to it here in the 1830's:

> Este cuento y apuesta son de Alciato. Cópialo Bowle [152: 519-6; Part II], quien cita igualmente para este propósito á la *Floresta española*. (Volume VI, p. 345).
> Trasposicion semejante á esta otra: *un poco venia diferentemente atado,* que se halla en la primera parte, como lo observa Bowle [158: 548-8; Part II]. (Volume VI, p. 407).
> Bowle enumera [163: 563-10; Part II] los poemas pastorales y composiciones sueltas de nuestros poetas en que se hallan estos nombres fingidos de pastoras, y cita á Virgilio en sus Bucólicas por lo relativo á *Amarilis, Galatea,* y *Filis*. (Volume VI, p. 441).

In this concluding chapter we have seen that Bowle's influence becomes widespread by the 1830's. Suffering sharp criticism when his work appeared, his method influences the later commentators tremendously. His basic approach is utilized, and many of the subjects he discusses and the sources he gives are also used. From Pellicer through Clemencín a gradual development is seen in the dissemination of the English editor's precepts. Pellicer is not at all ashamed of borrowing freely from what Bowle writes, in many cases failing to acknowledge the source of such material. This kind of approach changes with editors like Bastús and Clemencín, who combine the best of what Bowle does with a more personal insight into *Don Quixote*. Those writers like Quintana and Navarrete, while not producing editions of the novel as such, show the leadership of Bowle in the general opinions they express about Cervantes' work. Whether they criticize the English edition or not is immaterial. They are all guided by Bowle in some way. The type of investigation of *Don Quixote* started by Bowle has become an accepted part of Cervantean criticism by the 1820's and 1830's. When commentators like Bastús and Clemencín employ the same methods, many of the same sources, and even the same wording, they are in great part doing so unconsciously. Especially is this true of Clemencín, who criticizes Bowle for certain procedures on the one hand, and then uses these same procedures himself, falling into far more irritating habits of his own.

During these approximately fifty years, the 1781 edition suffers at times from unwarranted criticism and neglect. Yet in a more permanent fashion it wields such influence that its precepts become the essence of practically all later editions of *Don Quixote*. This influence is not one we find in attitudes or ideas about the characters of the novel. We do not expect to find Bowle at the forefront of any new interpretations of the "person" of Don Quixote, for example, although he does venture a few hesitant notions in this regard. Rather, we may say that Bowle is the real instigator of a totally new vision of *Don Quixote* and Cervantes. The editor's tremendous achievement is all the more outstanding when one reflects on how great a knowledge Bowle had to have of another country's language and customs before he could attempt to produce a work like his. Such knowledge and, even more so, such fruitful results were quite rare for his day. Even though the editor and his work have long been forgotten by the general public, Bowle has succeeded in his primary aims more than he ever believed possible.

In concluding this investigation of John Bowle's edition of *Don Quixote*, we may with complete justification recall the simple praise expressed by Julio Casares which was noted in the preface to this study. Bowle's "famosas 'anotaciones,' discutidas, mejoradas y con harta frecuencia saqueadas por quienes vinieron después, despiertan todavía admiración y pueden estudiarse con fruto." [3]

---

[3] Casares, p. 44.

BIBLIOGRAPHY

AMEZÚA Y MAYO, AGUSTÍN GONZÁLEZ DE. *Cervantes creador de la novela corta española*. Madrid, 1956.

———. "Cómo se hacía un libro en nuestro Siglo de Oro," *Bibliografía Hispánica*, V (Diciembre 1946), 761- 799.

ARMAS Y CÁRDENAS, JOSÉ DE. *Cervantes en la literatura inglesa*. Madrid, 1916.

ASHBEE, HENRY SPENCER. *Don Quixote and British Art*. London, 1900.

———. "Don Quixote and Pickwick," *Revue Hispanique*, VI (1899), 307-310.

ASHCOM, B. B. "A Note on Garcilaso and Cervantes," *Hispanic Review*, XIX (January 1951), 61-63.

ASTRANA MARÍN, LUIS. *Vida ejemplar y heroica de Cervantes Saavedra*. 7 vols. Madrid, 1948-1958.

BARDON, MAURICE. *"Don Quichotte" En France au XVII et au XVIII siècle 1605-1815*. 2 vols. Paris, 1931.

BARETTI, GIUSEPPE. *Tolondron*. London, 1786.

BASTÚS Y CARRERA, VICENTE JOAQUÍN. *Nuevas anotaciones al Ingenioso Hidalgo D. Quijote De La Mancha, de Miguel de Cervantes Saavedra*. Barcelona, 1834.

BEAUMONT, FRANCIS AND JOHN FLETCHER. *Comedies and Tragedies*. London, 1647.

———. *The Works of Francis Beaumont and John Fletcher*. 10 vols. London, 1905-1912.

BERTRAND, J.-J. A. *Cervantes Et Le Romantisme Allemand*. Paris, 1914.

BLAIR, HUGH. *Lectures on Rhetoric and Belles Lettres*, ed. Harold F. Harding. 2 vols. Carbondale, 1965.

BLECUA, JOSÉ MANUEL. "Garcilaso y Cervantes," *Cuadernos Insula*, I (1947), 141-150.

BONILLA Y SAN MARTÍN, ADOLFO. *De Crítica Cervantina*. Madrid, [1917].

BOSWELL, JAMES. *The Life of Samuel Johnson*. London, 1811.

BOUTERWEK, FREDERICK. *History of Spanish and Portuguese Literature*, trans. Thomasina Ross. London, 1823.

BOWLE, JOHN. *A Letter to the Reverend Dr. Percy, Concerning a New and Classical Edition of Historia Del Valeroso Cavallero Don Quixote De La Mancha*. London, 1777.

———. "Miscellaneous Observations on Parish Registers," *Archaeologia: or Miscellaneous Tracts Relating to Antiquity*, VIII (London 1781), 67-78.

BOWLE, JOHN. "Observations on Card-playing," *Archaeologia,* VIII (London 1781), 147-151.

———. *Remarks on the Extraordinary Conduct of the Knight of the Ten Stars, and His Italian Esquire, to the Editor of Don Quixote: in a Letter to the Rev. J.S.D.D.* London, 1785.

———. Several letters in the *Gentleman's Magazine.* LI, LIV, LV (London 1781, 1784, 1785).

———. For his edition of *Don Quixote,* see *Cervantes.*

BRADFORD, CARLOS F. *Índice de las notas de D. Diego Clemencín en su edición de El Ingenioso Hidalgo Don Quijote De La Mancha.* Madrid, 1885.

CADALSO, JOSÉ. *Cartas marruecas.* Buenos Aires, 1952.

CALDERÓN DE LA BARCA, PEDRO. *El alcalde de Zalamea.* Madrid: Espasa-Calpe, 1961.

CASARES, JULIO. "Las tres edades del 'Quijote,'" *Boletín de la Real Academia Española,* XXVII (Octubre 1947-Abril 1948), 43-60.

CASTRO Y BELLVÍS, GUILLÉN DE. *"Don Quixote De La Mancha," comedia en tres jornadas y en vers.* Valencia, 1905.

CERVANTES SAAVEDRA, MIGUEL DE. *Vida y hechos del ingenioso hidalgo Don Quixote de la Mancha.* Londres, 1738.

———. *El ingenioso hidalgo don Quixote de la Mancha.* Madrid, 1750. (There are two copies of this edition in the Hispanic Society of America, one of which contains the *Notas Ms. Tas.* of John Bowle's edition of *Don Quixote.*)

———. *El ingenioso hidalgo Don Quijote de la Mancha,* nueva edición corregida por la Real Academia Española, con la *Vida de Miguel de Cervantes, Análisis del Quixote, Plan cronológico del Quixote, Pruebas y documentos que justifican la vida de Cervantes* por Vicente de los Ríos. Madrid, 1780.

———. *Historia del famoso cavallero, Don Quixote de la Mancha,* con anotaciones, índices y varias lecciones por el Reverendo D. Juan Bowle. Salisbury, 1781.

———. ———. Londres, 1781.

———. *El ingenioso hidalgo Don Quixote de la Mancha,* nueva edición corregida ... por D. Juan Antonio Pellicer. Madrid, 1797-1798.

———. *El ingenioso hidalgo Don Quixote de la Mancha.* Madrid, 1797-1798. (This edition contains the unsigned essay on Cervantes by Manuel José Quintana.)

———. *El ingenioso hidalgo Don Quijote de la Mancha,* comentado por Don Diego Clemencín. Madrid, 1833-1839.

———. *El ingenioso hidalgo Don Quijote de la Mancha,* edición y notas de Francisco Rodríguez-Marín. (First Clásicos Castellanos edition of 8 vols. in 1911-1913.) Reprinted in 8 vols. in Madrid: I [1964], II [1961], III [1962], IV [1962], V [1964], VI [1957], VII [1962], VIII [1964].

———. *The History of Don Quichote,* trans. Thomas Shelton. 2 vols. London, 1620.

———. *The Life and Exploits of the Ingenious Gentleman Don Quixote de la Mancha,* trans. Charles Jarvis. London, 1742.

———. *Le Valevreux Don Quixote de la Mancha,* trans. César Oudin. Paris, 1616.

CERVANTES SAAVEDRA, MIGUEL DE. *Histoire De L'Admirable Don Quichotte de la Manche*, trans. Filleau de Saint-Martin. Paris, 1681.
CLEMENCÍN, DIEGO. See *Cervantes*.
COTARELO Y VALLEDOR, ARMANDO. *Cervantes lector*. Madrid, 1943.
The Dictionary of National Biography, ed. Sir Leslie Stephen and Sir Sidney Lee. London, 1921-1922.
DILLON, JOHN TALBOT. *Travels Through Spain*. London, 1780.
DOLDER, ERNST. *Henry Fielding's Don Quixote in England*. Zurich, 1907.
"The Enthusiasm of the Church of Rome, etc. L'Enthousiasme De L'Eglise romaine demontré par quelques remarques sur la vie d'*Ignace Loyola*," *Bibliothèque Universelle Et Historique De L'Année 1688*, XI (1702), 93-140.
FARQUHAR, GEORGE. *George Farquhar*, ed. William Archer. New York, 1959.
FERNÁNDEZ DE AVELLANEDA, ALONSO. *Ingenioso hidalgo Don Quixote de la Mancha*, Vol. 2. Tarragona, 1614.
FIELDING, HENRY. *The History of Tom Jones, a Foundling*. New York, [n. d.].
FITZMAURICE-KELLY, JAMES. *Cervantes and Shakespeare*. London, [1916].
FLORES, ÁNGEL AND M. J. BENARDETE. *Cervantes Across the Centuries*. New York, 1947.
GAYTON, EDMUND. *Pleasant Notes Upon Don Quixot* [sic], London, 1654.
———. *Festivous Notes on the History and Adventures of the Renowned Don Quixote*. London, 1768.
GOLDBERG, HOMER. "The Interpolated Stories in *Joseph Andrews* or 'The History of the World in General' Satirically Revised," *Modern Philology* LXIII (1966), 295-310.
GRANGER, JAMES. *A Biographical History of England, from Egbert the Great to the Revolution*. London, 1799.
———. *Letters Between the Rev. James Granger, M.A. Rector of Shiplake, and Many of the Most Eminent Literary Men of his Time*. London, 1805.
GRISMER, RAYMOND L. *Cervantes: A Bibliography*. Vol. I. Minneapolis, 1946, Vol. II, Minneapolis, 1963.
HERREO GARCÍA, MIGUEL. *Estimaciones literarias del siglo XVIII*. Madrid, 1930.
———. *Vida de Cervantes*. Madrid, 1948.
ICAZA, FRANCISCO A. DE. *El "Quijote" durante tres siglos*. Madrid, 1918.
ISLA, JOSÉ FRANCISCO DE. *Fray Gerundio de Campazas*, introducción y notas de Russell P. Sebold. Madrid, 1960-1964.
———. *La mojiganga teológica*. Madrid, 1930.
JOHNSON, SAMUEL. *Lives of the Poets*, ed. Mrs. Alexander Napier. London, 1890.
———. *The Rambler*, I. London, 1794.
JOVELLANOS, GASPAR MELCHOR DE. "Juicio crítico de un nuevo Quijote," *Obras escogidas*, III. Madrid, 1946.
KAMES, HENRY HOME OF. *Elements of Criticism*, ed. James R. Boyd. New York, Chicago, 1877.
KNOWLES, EDWIN B., JR. "A Note on Smollett's Don Quixote," *Modern Language Quarterly*, XVI (1955), 29-31.
———. "Cervantes and English Literature," *Cervantes Across the Centuries*, ed. Ángel Flores and M. J. Benardete. New York, 1947.

Knowles, Edwin B., Jr. "Don Quixote through English Eyes," *Hispania*, XXIII (1940), 103-115.

———. *Four Articles on Don Quixote in England*. New York, 1941.

———. "The First and Second Editions of Shelton's Don Quixote, Part I: A Collation and Dating," *Hispanic Review*, IX (1941), 252-265.

Linsalata, Carmine Rocco. *Smollett's Hoax: Don Quixote in English*. Stanford, 1956.

Lister, Jonn T. "A Comparison of Two Works of Cervantes with a Play by Massinger," *Hispania*, V (1922), 133-140.

Locke, John. *An Essay Concerning Human Understanding*, II. Boston, 1813.

López Estrada, Francisco. *"La Galatea" de Miguel de Cervantes, estudio crítico*. Las Palmas, 1948.

Menéndez y Pelayo, Marcelino. *Discurso acerca de Cervantes y el "Quijote."* Madrid, 1905.

The Monthly Review; or, Literary Journal, LXXIII (from July to December inclusive). London, 1786.

Navarrete, Martín Fernández de. *Vida de Miguel de Cervantes Saavedra*. Barcelona, 1834.

Nichols, John. *Illustrations of the Literary History of the Eighteenth Century*. London, 1831.

———. *Literary Anecdotes of the Eighteenth Century Comprising Biographical Memoirs of William Bowyer, Printer, F.S.A. and Many of His Learned Friends*. London, 1812.

Nicolas, Sir Nicholas Harris. *The Letters of Joseph Ritson*. London, 1833.

Le Novelle Antiche, con una introduzione sulla storia esterna del testo del Novellino per Guido Biagi. Firenze, [n.d.].

Libro Di Novelle, et di bel parlar gentile, nel qual si contengono Cento Nouelle altrauolta mandate fuori da Messer Carlo Gualteruzzi da Fano. Fiorenza, 1572.

The Oxford Companion to Classical Literature, ed. Sir. Paul Harvey. Oxford, 1940.

Pane, Remigio U. *English Translations from the Spanish, 1484-1943. A Bibliography*. New Brunswick, 1944.

Parker, A. A. "Fielding and the Structure of *Don Quixote*," *Bulletin of Hispanic Studies*, XXXIII (1956), 1-16.

Peers, E. Allison. "Aportación de los hispanistas extranjeros al estudio de Cervantes," *Revista de filología española*, XXXII (1948), 151-188.

———. "Cervantes ante Inglaterra," *Saint Teresa of Jesus and Other Essays and Addresses*. London, 1953.

———. "Cervantes in England," *Bulletin of Spanish Studies*, XXIV (1948), 226-238.

———. "Cervantes en Inglaterra," *Homenaje a Cervantes*, ed. Francisco Sánchez-Castañer. 2 vols. Valencia, 1950.

Pellicer, Juan Antonio. See *Cervantes*.

Percy, Thomas, Bishop of Dromore. *Reliques of Ancient English Poetry, Consisting of Old Heroic Ballads, Songs, and Other Pieces of Our Earlier Poets*. London, 1847.

Quintana, Manuel José. See *Cervantes*.

RANDALL, DALE B. J. *The Golden Tapestry. A Critical Survey of Nonchivalric Spanish Fiction in English Translation* (1543-1657). Durham, 1963.
REAL DE LA RIVA, CÉSAR. "Historia de la crítica e interpretación de la obra de Cervantes," *Revista de filología española*, XXXII (1948), 107-150.
RÍO Y RICO, GABRIEL MARTÍN DEL. *Catálogo bibliográfico de la sección de Cervantes de la Biblioteca Nacional*. Madrid, 1930.
RÍOS, VICENTE DE LOS. See *Cervantes*.
RIUS, LEOPOLDO. *Bibliografía crítica de las obras de Miguel de Cervantes Saavedra*. Madrid, 1895.
RODRÍGUEZ-MARÍN, FRANCISCO. *La cárcel en que se engendró el "Quijote."* Madrid, 1916.
———. For his edition of *Don Quixote*, see *Cervantes*.
SERÍS, HOMERO. "La colección Cervantina de la Sociedad Hispánica de América," *University of Illinois Studies in Language and Literature*, VI. Urbana, 1920.
SIMONDE DE SISMONDI, J. C. L. *De la Littérature Du Midi de l'Europe*. Paris, 1819.
STARKIE, WALTER. "Cervantes y la novela inglesa," *Homenaje a Cervantes*, ed. Francisco Sánchez-Castañer. 2 vols. Valencia, 1950.
TAVE, STUART M. *The Amiable Humorist*. Chicago, 1960.
TÉLLEZ, GABRIEL. *Comedias escogidas de Fray Gabriel Téllez*. Madrid, 1850.
TICKNOR, GEORGE. *History of Spanish Literature*. 3 vols. London, 1849.
———. ———. New York, 1854.
[TORRES VILLARROEL, DIEGO]. Nicolás De Molani Nogui Interiano [pseud.]. *Qverella que Don Quixote De La Mancha da en el tribunal de la mverte contra Don Francisco de Quevedo, sobre la primera, y segunda parte de Las Visiones y Visitas de Don Diego De Torres*. Madrid, [n.d.].
VOLTAIRE. *Œuvres Complètes De Voltaire, Correspondance*, II, nouvelle édition conforme pour le texte à l'édition de Beuchot. Paris, 1880.
———. *Œuvres Complètes De Voltaire*, I, *Dictionnaire Philosophique*, eds. Emile De La Bédollière et Georges Avenel. Paris, 1867.
WILSON, EDWARD M. "Cervantes and English Literature of the Seventeenth Century," *Bulletin Hispanique*, L, i (1948), 27-52.
———. "Edmund Gayton on Don Quixote, Andrés, and Juan Haldudo," *Comparative Literature*, II (1950), 64-72.

www.ingramcontent.com/pod-product-compliance
Lightning Source LLC
Chambersburg PA
CBHW020420230426
43663CB00007BA/1253